Transport Economics & Policy

Also by John Hibbs and published by Kogan Page

The Bus and Coach Operator's Handbook
An Introduction to Transport Studies, 3rd edition

Other transport titles from Kogan Page

Applied Transport Economics, 2nd edition
Stuart Cole

The Certificate of Professional Competence, 3rd edition
David Lowe

The Dangerous Goods Safety Manual
David Lowe

The Dictionary of Transport and Logistics
David Lowe

Global Logistics and Distribution Planning, 4th edition
Edited by Donald Waters

A Guide to the Large Goods Vehicle Driving Licence, Driving Test and Theory Test,
    10th edition
David Lowe

The Handbook of Logistics and Distribution Management, 2nd edition
Alan Rushton, John Oxley and Phil Croucher

International Transport, 5th edition
Rex Faulks

Logistics and Retail Management
Edited by John Fernie and Leigh Sparks

Managing Passenger Logistics
Paul Fawcett

The Pocket Guide to LGV Drivers' Hours and Tachograph Law
David Lowe

A Practical Guide to Planning and Operation
Brian Marchant

A Study Manual of Professional Competence in Road Haulage, 10th edition
David Lowe

The Transport Manager's and Operator's Handbook 2003, 33rd edition
David Lowe

Transport Economics & Policy

A Practical Analysis of Performance, Efficiency and Marketing Objectives

JOHN HIBBS

The Institute of
Logistics and Transport

KOGAN
PAGE

London and Sterling, VA

Appendix 2 is an amended and updated version of a *Glossary of Economic and Related Terms: For the use of students on transport courses*, first published in 1993 by Roadmaster Publishing.

First published in Great Britain and the United States in 2003 by Kogan Page Limited

120 Pentonville Road
London N1 9JN
UK
www.kogan-page.co.uk

22883 Quicksilver Drive
Sterling VA 20166-2012
USA

ISBN 0 7494 3772 3

British Library Cataloguing-in-Publication Data

A CIP record for this book is available from the British Library.

Typeset by JS Typesetting Ltd, Wellingborough, Northants
Printed and bound in Great Britain by Biddles Ltd, Guildford and King's Lynn
www.biddles.co.uk

*Dedicated to the memory of
Arthur Lainson, Gilbert Ponsonby and Alec Tait
from whom I learnt so much*

Contents

Foreword

In 1975 I was at a management seminar being held by a National Bus Company subsidiary to discuss the impact of the new funding for transport introduced by the 1972 Local Government Act. 'What this means for us', said one of the directors, 'is that we can stop worrying about the quantity of service, and concentrate on the quality.'

As a young manager on my first posting, I did not challenge the statement. But it jarred, which is probably why I remember it so well. It seemed to me an abdication of responsibility: matching service demand and supply was a fundamental management task, and leaving it to outsiders seemed ludicrous.

It was symptomatic of the times though: the industry was grappling with the problems of decline, whilst policy-makers were coming to see buses as no more than a backstop for those unable to afford a car yet. Public subsidy, as opposed to enhanced customer appeal, was seen as the answer and embraced enthusiastically. We now know, of course, that it all ended in tears.

I was suspicious even in 1975, perhaps because I had been taught transport economics by John Hibbs. Looking back, that teaching was crucial to my subsequent thinking and I'm sure I am not alone.

We heard views, trenchantly but entertainingly expressed, founded on intellectually rigorous analysis. In the 1970s, some of his views were unfashionable: today, a market-based approach to passenger transport is more widely (but alas not universally) accepted.

This book presents John's teaching to a wider audience. The views remain trenchant and intellectually rigorous, while the issues addressed are just as topical, and the same economic principles apply.

A good example is the discussion on road pricing in Chapters 6 and 8. The economist's approach to this key question in the transport policy debate provides a fascinating insight, particularly on the market distortion that results from road space remaining free at the point of use.

Ultimately, good management and planning in transport come from an understanding of the basic tenets, applying those concepts in a rigorous analysis, and then acting accordingly. Whether you are a transport professional or a student, and whether you are in freight or passenger, road or rail, or in tourism, the structure of this book is itself an object lesson in how to do just that. The contents are fascinating and will be invaluable. Read and use the book now. More importantly, return to it regularly and clear your mind of the fog of day-to-day events. It will be a rewarding experience.

Christopher Cheek
Director, The TAS Partnership Ltd

Preface

The transport industry occupies a special place in people's minds, and public debate seems to suggest that it is not well understood. A career in the industry, first in management and then in teaching and research about it, has convinced me that a framework based in economics can be the foundation for a more rigorous understanding, which is what is attempted here. The approach is first, in Part One, to establish the central concepts of economics in a transport-related discussion. This then forms a 'template' which in Part Two is tested against the principal modes of inland transport in Great Britain, and in the relationship between transport and tourism. The importance of marketing management for the transport industries is examined in Part Three, in terms of the efficiency and effectiveness of service industries; and the conclusion, in Part Four, is critical of the idea that there might be some perfection that could be planned for. Rather, the future is unknowable, and the market solution is preferable to the administrative solution in tending to the solution of the transport problem.

I am most grateful to my colleagues, Alasdair Traill and David Gillingwater, who suggested that I should make a book out of the courses I developed for them at Aston and Loughborough Universities, and to Paul Truelove and Melvyn Hopwood for their contributions by way of correction and improvement. The preparation of this book has benefitted greatly by discussion with colleagues and students, and especially with Kevin Hey of Salford University, and my research student Paul Kevill. Peter Huggins, Librarian of the Institute of Logistics and Transport, gave me valuable assistance in identifying books, magazines and Web sites. As ever I am indebted to my wife and family for putting up with a writer about the house.

I must emphasize that the argument, along with any faults or errors, remains solely my own responsibility.

John Hibbs
University of Central England
January 2003

Part one

The economic issues

1

The basic concepts revisited

ECONOMICS IS ABOUT HUMAN BEHAVIOUR IN CIRCUMSTANCES OF SCARCITY

Over human history this has turned upon the exchange of relatively scarce items, at first by barter or gifts between elites, and then, when money was invented, by bargaining, with prices representing relative scarcities. Bargaining takes place in a market, which may be physical, but which for most purposes is the set of cash relationships that exist in a community, which may be large or small, and is increasingly world-wide. Some 200 years ago an economist coined the word 'catallactics' to describe what goes on in the market, from which we have the term 'catallaxy', to describe a human process whose origin is lost in history and which has no narrowly scientific status.

Cash-based bargains should never be 'zero-sum' – unless there is ignorance or undue influence on one side or the other, each party is left feeling better off. But price alone does not account for the 'buy/not-buy' decisions that we all make, all the time, in the market; our decisions reflect a trade-off between price and quality. We would all like to go to work in a chauffer-driven luxury car, but we settle for a season ticket on the bus or train because that represents, for us, better value for money. Each of us has his or her own assessment of what represents better value, although this may be coloured by relative ignorance of the prices and qualities on offer, but each decision we take is one of many millions of signals that go to make up the market process, from which producers identify what it is that we want and are willing to pay for, and seek to provide a supply.

The market is a spontaneous phenomenon that has grown up because people have found it useful. It could never be designed. Between the two world wars there took place what was called the 'calculation debate', between economists who thought you could second-guess demand and supply and run a 'managed market' that would be as efficient as the traditional one, and others who argued that it could never work. It was tried under Stalin and in the former Soviet economies, and it clearly did not work; but today we have the contribution of chaos theory and what is called non-linear dynamics, which demonstrate that it could not work. There are of course many cases where the market does not work all that well – we call them market failures, a subject to which we shall return.

The function of the market, and therefore the aim of economic policy, is to achieve two essential objectives: the efficient allocation of scarce resources of all kinds, combined with the satisfaction of effective consumer demand. 'Efficiency' is not used here as an engineer would use the term; what is efficient is best described as what is optimal, in balancing all the different expressions of demand that are shown by our decisions in the market. 'Effective' demand is demand that is backed up with purchasing power and willingness to pay. The market process tends to a trade-off between these two desirable objectives, which is always a compromise, with no perfect solution that can be achieved at any point in time. For the future is always unknowable (but see 'Discount', below).

For the market to tend to efficiency and effectiveness it must be open. A 'perfect market', were such a thing to exist, would require perfect knowledge of all that is going on, which is impossible; but what is more important is how open it is, a condition that we call its contestability. How easy is it to enter, and, just as important, how easy is it to leave? (Entry might not be attractive if there were barriers to leaving if the business were not a success.) One big barrier to exit, and therefore to entry, is the existence of substantial sunk costs (see below). What factors might constrain the working of the trade-off, especially the existence of government intervention? In a fully contestable market, which may not often exist, there should be the opportunity for new competitors to appear, take a profit, and get out promptly – what might be called 'hit and run' competition.

In the real world neither suppliers nor consumers always like competition. Company directors and business managers often prefer a monopoly – not so much because of the wealth they seek as because 'the greatest monopoly profit is a quiet life', without having to look over your shoulder all the time to see if some new competitor threatens you. They set up cartels (see below) or they bargain with the government for statutory protection. Consumers today find it increasingly difficult to decide what is value for money, or they may be too busy to make comparisons, while to bargain is socially unacceptable (at least in Britain). In large businesses departmental managers may seek their own objectives, which can conflict with the best interests of the firm, while all forms of government intervention are subject to regulatory failure, often because administrators, too, have their own agenda to pursue, or because elected representatives intervene to seek votes. Even the necessary regulation for safety in fail-dangerous industries like transport may suffer from these problems. (Your domestic electricity circuit should be 'fail-safe' – if anything goes wrong it blows a fuse. But if the brakes on a car fail in traffic, you know what to expect – they are 'fail-dangerous'.)

To understand the transport industry, and its economics, it is important to make a distinction between movement and infrastructure; between the vehicles and vessels on the one hand, and the 'track, terminals and signalling' that they require for purposes of movement. This is a subject to which we shall return.

RISK, PRODUCTION AND THE ENTREPRENEUR

Because of the inherent uncertainties of the market process – the 'unknowable future' – all decisions that are not necessarily 'on the spot' require an element of second-guessing what the future may hold. It is here that the element of risk comes in, and the greater the risk, the greater the reward. This is where the entrepreneur, or 'enterpriser', comes in, as we shall see in Chapter 5. The product of transport firms is safe arrival (of passengers) or safe delivery (of goods) in accordance with a time schedule (if one exists). This product can be measured in terms of seat-miles or capacity tonne-miles, but, because it is impossible to store, if it is not sold in the moment of production it is wasted. (Think of empty seats on a bus.) This is what makes the element of risk so important, for no one wants to see production running to waste, and that is why we shall see how important marketing is, in Part Three.

What the entrepreneur brings to the market is a quality we may call flair, in arriving at investment and pricing decisions. Without entrepreneurs the market cannot function – there is no place for them in so-called planned economy, yet they will appear even there, exploiting the failures of the system, albeit in a criminal capacity. Entrepreneurs function to bring supply and demand into balance at levels of price and quality that will satisfy both buyers and sellers, and they tend in this way to restore equilibrium in a distorted market.

Producers, helped along by entrepreneurs, combine the factors of production (land, labour and capital) so as to seek a profit in trade. Land means all physical resources; labour means all human effort, mental or physical; and capital is accumulated wealth, constantly enhanced (since the 15th century) by compound interest. Consumers judge the price and quality of the goods and services on offer in the market, and make their own buy/not-buy decisions. The entrepreneur also bridges the gap between what is on offer and what consumers might buy if new products became available. All these signals are constantly circulating in the market, and it is inconceivable that any organization could bring all this data together for decision making at one place and time (and even then, it would have been long out of date). The signals then tend to determine prices, which relate to the 'marginal utility' of each item to the buyer – as much as the buyer is willing to pay for one more unit of output, be it an apple or a bus ride.

CONSUMER COSTS AND ELASTICITIES

The price of goods and services will be determined by the producer. To the consumer, the price is seen as part of the cost, and this will determine whether or not he or she is willing to buy. (The same principle applies to freight forwarding and physical distribution.) We call this 'generalized cost', which is a mix of money price and disutility. Walking to the bus stop and waiting for the bus is a disutility, especially if it is raining, and so are unreliable train services. In manufacturing, managers are generally better informed about the price and quality of transport, and they can negotiate terms in advance. One result of all this is that you may find your choice cheaper than an alternative, even at a higher money price.

There is a further problem here for the working of the market, which is the extent to which buy/not-buy decisions are based on perceived cost, rather than the actual figures involved. Few of us know or care about the real cost of using a car (and in the absence of road-use pricing, we cannot know this). But if you always use a car you will be ignorant of the money costs of going by train or bus, leave alone the relative disutilities. So it is hard to treat private and public transport as substitutes, since they are in practice competitors, and that means that the relative elasticities of demand mean little in practice.

Elasticities of demand (see Appendix 1) reflect the extent to which it is likely that consumers will buy more or less of any product, if either the price goes down (or the quality rises at the same price) or the price goes up (or the quality goes down at the same price), or there is any change in the mix of price and quality. Accurate figures are hard to forecast (we really only know after the change has taken place, when it is too late), but they are central for the decision making of the risk-taking entrepreneur, and often it is flair that must be used to attempt a forecast. Elasticities in the passenger market vary widely, by time of day, day of week, and time of year, as well as by market segment; this last being a factor often neglected today. In the freight market elasticities vary with the state of the economy and also with investment in the infrastructure.

PRODUCERS' COSTS

Traffic costing has been said to be more of an art than a science, but the secret is to know what costs need to be taken into account for what decisions. Thus labour costs around 60 per cent of movement costs for most branches of transport, but we may ignore this for some decisions concerning vehicle mileage within the guaranteed working day, when we would be paying the staff any way. Thus we distinguish between fixed and escapable costs, but with the reservation, fixed within what period? We also distinguish joint and common costs: an example of the former being the relationship between the outward and homeward journey, while cost-centre costs may be common to all vehicles working from the same depot. For practical purposes it may help if we define a rising scale, from micro-costing (whether to add an extra journey or another drop on a distribution schedule) through route costing to cost-centre costing and thus to the cost of staying in business. Average costing, which allocates all costs on a per-vehicle-mile basis, is misleading for most practical purposes, although 'at the end of the day' average revenue must meet and exceed average cost.

The concept of profit must be clearly defined in this context. Revenue must exceed total outgoings, including interest payments, but must also provide for the replacement costs of the firm's assets, as well as allowing for their earning power (see 'Opportunity costs', below). Only when these matters have been taken into account does profit come in: not of course as a cost, but as a measure that attracts entrepreneurship. With no potential profit, what is the point of taking risk?

Suppliers will seek to meet these conditions by setting prices to the extent to which they are free to do so. In principle the price for transport will be set according to what the traffic will bear; that is, the highest price the provider can get away with, subject to either attracting new competition or discouraging demand. But economies of scale (see below) may reduce unit cost (cost per unit of output), so that customer prices can come down even though total operating costs are higher. (The civil aviation industry has developed in this way.)

Pricing becomes more complex where there are substantial sunk costs, representing large investments in assets with a long life, and often with a lengthy delivery period. Merchant ships and aircraft are good examples, and so also are sea and airports, railways, roads and bridges. Pricing failures here may cause severe distortions in the economy; roads are not priced at all, while shipping earnings may be set so low in a period of recession as to discourage further investment. Linked with this is the problem of inventory costs, which arises when we have to decide what stocks of spare parts or spare vehicles we can afford to retain. If replacements can be bought quickly it may be possible to avoid substantial overhead costs.

Not all of the company's costs are 'brought to book'; they are not directly paid for. These 'external costs' have to be met from other sources, usually the taxpayer. Pollution (including noise), congestion (costs imposed on others) and the uninsured costs of accidents (including hospital treatment) are all examples. Attempts are always being made to internalize such costs, for example by requiring road vehicles to be fitted with expensive anti-pollution devices, but this is a highly political area. Suggestions that 'social exclusion' (poverty) should be seen as an externality raise severe problems of measurement.

Production is also affected by economies of scale and economies of scope. Economies of scale occur when each additional unit of production costs less than the previous one, generally because fixed or overhead costs can be spread over a greater volume of production. Another source is the extent to which certain requirements, such as fuel and insurance, can cost less if bought in bulk. But it does not follow that a firm can go on expanding without limit; diseconomies of scale set in, typical examples being weak marketing management and customer care, and the tendency for separate departments to pursue objectives that conflict with each other, and with the success of the firm. Claims that there are network benefits (as externalities) in passenger transport are very hard to quantify. Economies of scope arise where two firms or two cost centres can be merged, giving better use of the assets without significantly increasing the overhead or fixed costs. This can be a real advantage, but here again the process ends when diseconomies of scale set in. It has been well said that a small railway is easier to manage than a big one, and this may help to account for the absence of many large-scale firms in the road freight business and in the coaching trade.

Finally, there is the matter of opportunity cost, which is the key to deciding whether or not to stay in business, or in any specific part of the market. This may be expressed by saying that an opportunity foregone is a cost. If the firm's capital, or some part of it, could earn more in another line of business, or if the assets could be sold and the money could earn more if it were invested in long-term government securities, then there is an indication for escape. For many small firms, though, there are non-monetary satisfactions which mean that the proprietor is happy for the assets to earn less than the marginal rate. But opportunity cost becomes very important when deciding on the replacement of assets (ships, trains, road vehicles or aircraft), and they will figure centrally in decisions about new investment. Here the calculation of discounted cash flow (DCF) or net present value (NPV) enables us to forecast the relative benefits to be expected from longer-term investment, and firms may use it as a 'target rate of return'. A simple example is set out in Figure 1.1.

CONCLUSION

The concept of opportunity cost presents us with the question 'Would we be better off without it?', and this may be applied to each unit of output, as well as to the buy/not-buy decisions of the consumer. Ultimately it is all about value for money. And this brings us back to the catallaxy; to the function of the market, which is to tend to the efficient allocation of scarce resources by and through the satisfaction of effective consumer demand. While there can be

Figure 1.1 Allowing for discount

The choice lies between vehicle A, costing £5000 and vehicle B, costing £6000. The discount rate to be used is 8% compound. We set out our estimates in a table:

Vehicle A Year	Estimated earnings	Discounted earnings @ 8%	Vehicle B Estimated earnings	Discounted earnings @ 8%
1	£2000	£1852	£2000	£1852
2	£3000	£2571	£3000	£2571
3	£3000	£2382	£4000	£3176
4	£2000	£1470	£3000	£2205
		£8275		£9804

Note: The discounted value of £1 at 8% compound for each of the four years is as follows:

Year	Year 1	Year 2	Year 3	Year 4
Value	£0.926	£0.857	£0.794	£0.735

We now deduct the initial outlay from the discounted income to arrive at the net present value of the two vehicles:

Vehicle	Discounted income	Initial outlay	Net present value
Vehicle A	£8275 −	£5000 =	£3275
Vehicle B	£9804 −	£6000 =	£3804

Thus the choice is vehicle B, despite the higher first cost.

no ideal outcome of this process, if only because the future is unknown and to a great extent unknowable, there are seen to be two ways to deal with the problem: the administrative solution and the market solution, which we shall return to in Chapter 18. Both theory and experience suggest that the market solution does the better job, but where there are market failures the administrative solution may be required; even though this brings up the problem that there are administrative failures as well.

In the following chapters we shall use the principles we have discussed here, to identify these economic issues, and to see how the use of economics can help us to understand them. Then in Part Two we shall apply them to each mode of transport in turn, and analyse its efficiency and effectiveness.

Questions for discussion

1. What makes a market contestable, and why does it matter if it is?
2. Could there ever be a 'correct' price for any commodity?
3. What is meant by 'opportunity cost'?

2

The importance of costing

TRAFFIC COSTING IS FUNDAMENTAL FOR SUCCESS

Because of the perishability of the transport product, it is extremely important to understand the costs in the process that ends (hopefully) with a satisfied customer. While manufacturing is increasingly automated, service industries in general are labour-intensive, and transport is no exception.

Standard accounting practice distinguishes first of all between fixed and variable costs. Fixed costs (sometimes called 'overheads') must be incurred if there is to be any output. They may include sunk costs, which cannot be recovered even if production ceases. Examples are sea and air ports and railway track, especially the tube railways. Variable costs depend upon the level of output. Drivers in the road freight and passenger sectors, aircraft and ship's crews are obvious examples, but maintenance of track and terminals can vary in their staff requirements according to the needs of traffic, and so can the need for booking clerks and check-in staff at airports. What is fixed and what is variable depends also upon the length of time involved; in the long run more costs are variable and fewer are fixed. The importance of opportunity cost we examined in Chapter 1, and the subject of track costs, while it is of vital importance, will be discussed in Part Two, Chapter 8.

Small businesspeople need to know their costs if they are to survive, but they need also to understand them. The great railway companies of the British Isles, from the start until after the Second World War, had a confused and inadequate understanding of their costs, which weakened their allocative efficiency. Price control in the bus industry from 1931 led to serious weaknesses in costing practice, which undermined the efficiency of that industry too. In the highly competitive road freight industry firms could not afford such mistakes, and in the absence of price control such problems did not arise.

After 1950 the British Transport Costing Service started to analyse the costs of railway and road transport operations, and it became clear that much railway traffic was not earning anything like enough to cover its costs. From this the concept of traffic costing developed, and this lies at the heart of good management practice for all modes of transport. The key to understanding it is to ensure that you understand why you need to know the costs you are looking for.

WOULD WE BE BETTER OFF WITHOUT IT?

We shall see when we look at pricing in the next chapter how important it is to make sure that revenue is sufficient to cover the costs that we can only avoid by ceasing to provide the service or services concerned. But these 'inescapable' costs will vary according to the decisions that we need to take. If a driver is paid for a guaranteed day's work, and you can fit an extra journey into his or her schedule, the wages paid are not escapable, so you would not have to take them into account when you reach your decision. At the opposite extreme, if you are deciding whether to stay in business then all costs are escapable. You might say that the decision about the extra trip is microcosting, but everything turns upon what costs you could escape if you did not provide a service. The box gives an example of the process.

SHOULD WE FLY OR SHOULD WE NOT?

An airline has an Airbus standing idle at a British airport between morning and evening trips. What costs would have to be covered if the airline were to schedule it to fly to Amsterdam and back? If the crew would otherwise spend the day in the canteen, then labour cost cannot be escaped, so you do not include it, and that, as we have seen, may be 60 per cent of the total costs for the trip, leaving 40 per cent to be covered by revenue. (But remember two things: first, you should aim to do better than this; and second, if it turns out that Brussels would be a more attractive destination, then you must switch to Brussels as soon as you can.)

HOW TO UNDERSTAND COSTS AND MAKE COST SAVINGS

Cutting costs by means of microcosting can risk damaging the business. A municipal tramway manager in the inter-war years sought to make savings by cutting each line back every so often, until the system was no longer financially viable. Whether in distribution or bus services you have to 'take the rough with the smooth', and though there may be few passengers or parcels at the outer end of the trip, they will have made their contribution to the cost of the journey. (Airlines try to avoid the problem by scheduling their flights from point to point, without too many intermediate stops.) The box on page 16 shows how dangerous it is to concentrate on cost savings without considering the quality of the service.

It is generally best to look for cost savings by means of cost-centre costing. A cost centre may be a depot or any part of the firm that can be identified as incurring specific costs. Where coaches and buses work from the same garage it may be worthwhile to identify each vehicle as a distinct cost centre, and the same might apply where tippers are working away from base on a construction contract. When British Railways withdrew steam locomotives,

---

SAVINGS CAN DEFEAT THEIR OWN PURPOSE

In 1968 the Ministry of Transport, with the support of the bus industry, altered the Construction and Use Regulations to permit the introduction of rear-engine vehicles. This was intended to allow more seats, and to do away with the need for a conductor. The outcome was a loss of revenue. One reason was that driver-only (one-person operated) buses could not provide the valued help and attention of the conductor, but also the increased size meant that fewer buses were needed to provide a given quantity of seats, and so frequencies were often reduced. Frequency, market research shows, is one of the things people value most in bus services.

---

which required daily maintenance, substantial savings arose from the closure of surplus depots, although there were examples of failure to achieve the savings where steam and diesel locomotives worked from the same depot, leading to two cost centres existing where only one would otherwise have been required. Savings of this kind may need to be offset against additional mileage, but accounting techniques exist for cost-centre costing, and considerable benefits arise when they are practised effectively.

The remaining area for analysis and control is to be met with in central costs: the overhead costs involved in keeping the firm in business. These can be divided between staff costs and fixed overheads, such as buildings and engineering equipment. Staff costs include everyone engaged in management, as distinct from operations, and in today's 'lead' businesses there will be pressure to keep these appointments to a minimum. (In municipal and publicly owned businesses this may not be so firmly applied.) Both types of cost apply where stocks (of spare parts and so on) have to be carried, and where the control of inventory cost is important. As in manufacturing, the idea of just-in-time provision of what is needed means a minimum of warehousing. Inventory cost however must be balanced against the cost of downtime, which occurs when a vehicle, ship or aircraft is out of service while awaiting maintenance or repair.

Finally we must consider the uses and dangers of average costs, which we shall return to when we look at pricing in the next chapter. To arrive at the average cost per kilometre we take the total costs for the firm and divide them by the number of kilometres operated. (The figures will of course apply to the year previous to the one we are in at the time.) From our discussion of costs that may be escapable you will see how dangerous it is to use average cost as the only measure of success or failure in the case of any section of output. We must also remember that for the firm to survive, its average costs must be more than covered by average revenue when the accounts are made up at the end of the year. These costs must include the replacement cost of the firm's assets, and also an estimate of opportunity costs (see Chapter 1), while the extra must be the desired element of profit (but opportunity cost and profit will not be included for municipal businesses).

THE COSTS WE DO NOT MEET

When all has been added up ('brought to book', we say), there remain serious cost items that do not appear on the profit and loss account. These give rise to problems that we shall examine in Chapter 6, but we must take note of them here.

First there are the problems of externalities. These are costs that transport operation imposes upon other people and other businesses. The most obvious is pollution of the atmosphere, which adds up to a very large sum for the economy as a whole, expressed in terms of illness and lost time. Alongside of it there is damage to the physical environment, such as happens where heavy traffic weakens the foundations of buildings at the roadside. Some would argue for government intervention to set the balance straight, but we shall see in Chapter 5 that there are serious problems with this.

Second, there are the problems for road transport of all kinds that arise from the way in which the infrastructure is financed, since the taxation that is an internal cost bears no relationship to the cost of building and maintaining roads. There may also be external benefits, where consumers gain something that they do not pay for, but these are difficult to define, and tend also to have political significance, which we shall examine in Chapter 7.

LOSS-MAKING SERVICES

No business can survive for long with a 'negative cash flow', and at the end of the financial year the firm's income must have been at least sufficient to provide for its outgoings. Above that there is the need to provide for the replacement of assets, and to maintain a reserve fund against unforeseen emergencies. Income from vehicle mileage must therefore be sufficient to cover costs per vehicle mile, with a sufficient positive margin.

The problem with this is that units of output (vehicle miles) vary considerably in the revenue that they provide. Commuter trains in the morning come into the city stations packed with people, but they leave almost empty, so season ticket prices have to reflect this. When a truck has delivered its cargo to a firm in another city it has to return empty, unless another load can be obtained. This gives rise to the 'back load problem', where the owner will seek a load at cut price, since the costs of the return trip are zero; but this undermines the market for operators in the distant city.

On the whole the market sorts these problems out over time, but in one area the market was prevented for a century or more from working freely in this way. When the Victorian railway companies were perceived to have a monopoly, parliament intervened to control their prices, and at the same time it was assumed that they ought to provide some services at a loss, and subsidize them out of profits made elsewhere in the system. This was known as internal cross-subsidy, and since fares and freight rates were set by the government, the outcome was totally to distort the market. The growth of commercial motor transport meant that the cross-subsidy was no longer justified, but it remained central to transport policy until it was progressively abandoned for the railways after 1962. Extended to bus services after 1931, it led to disastrous management policy (as we shall see in Chapter 10) until it was abandoned in 1985.

The principle that was neglected in this argument is that all mileage must at least cover the escapable costs involved, as we indicated earlier in this chapter. This does not prohibit the occasional 'loss leader', but it is always important to know what the costs are for each management decision. Thus within the guaranteed day even wage costs may not count. Above this 'floor' each unit of output will bring varying levels of remuneration, all contributing to the fixed and overhead costs of the business. Prices, as we shall see in Chapter 3, must then be set so as to ensure that escapable costs are met, and then to gain as much net revenue as possible, the ceiling being the point at which demand falls, either because customers no longer value the product, or through the entry of new competitors charging lower prices.

CONCLUSION

In many small transport firms the proprietor knows pretty well what the costs are, and works out what each vehicle needs to earn per day in order to stay in business. It is a rough-and-ready system, but it will not work for anything but the smallest business, and one where the manager has the figures at his or her fingertips. Where price competition is strong, as it is over most of the transport industry today, a better understanding and more accurate knowledge of costs is essential; but as we said at the start of the chapter, you must always know what sort of cost data you need for whatever decision you have to take.

Questions for discussion

1. Are wages a micro or a macro cost?
2. When do average costs matter?
3. What is meant by inescapable costs?

3

The importance of pricing

PRICING IS MORE OF AN ART THAN A SCIENCE

Prices in the market are set by producers in response to what consumers indicate is an acceptable rate at a given level of quality, and both price and quality are adjusted in the process. There can be no single 'right' price for any commodity, whether it is an article for sale, or a contract for negotiation, or any unit of output of the transport industry. Attempts to arrive at prices by calculation inevitably fail, which was one of the principal reasons for the collapse of the Soviet economic system in Russia, Eastern Europe and elsewhere. Elasticities, as we have seen, are difficult to forecast, and customers' tastes change where quality is concerned, and when they are presented with improvements in technology. The freedom for prices to fluctuate in the market, reflecting relative scarcities as well as changes in demand, is central to the efficient working of the catallaxy. As any domestic purchaser knows, this may mean that what appear to be close substitutes will be available at different prices in different shops, and businesses in the supply chain will expect to find a range of prices on offer from the distribution specialists.

Customers, on the other hand, prefer a degree of stability in prices, and this limits the freedom of management to adjust to changes in the market. In a contestable market there will always be competitors who are prepared to go below the current price levels, perhaps because they have lower costs, or just so as to make a quick profit and get out. The manager must have a close knowledge, not only of the firm's own costs, but also of the going rate for similar traffic where competitors are concerned. With experience a manager should acquire a sense of 'what the market will bear', and this is indeed a key quality for the success of the transport firm.

All of this shows the importance of giving transport management the greatest possible freedom in setting prices, at given levels of quality of service. Yet there has often been pressure for them to be fixed, or controlled. Parliament introduced statutory control of railway rates and charges toward the end of the 19th century, and this meant that railway managers had no freedom to compete with commercial motor transport as it developed after 1919. This played no small a part in the growing financial crisis of the railways, and it was not removed until 1962, by which time the nationalized railway had become insolvent. Road freight carriers' rates have never been subject to control, and that part of the industry has always been able to pay its way. Price control of bus and coach services (but not charter hire) was introduced in 1930 with no real thought being given to the consequences, the result being that managers were unable to meet the fast-expanding competition of the private car after 1950, and the provision of services declined, with increasing need for subsidy from taxation. Control of fares was removed in 1980, and here again the industry has since been able to pay its way.

THE ECONOMIC CONSEQUENCES OF SUBSIDY

Subsidy may take two forms, each of them having significant consequences for the market process. The older of the two is known as internal cross-subsidy (see the box on page 23), which means that parts of the business which produce greater revenue are expected to subsidize other parts, where demand is less. (This used to be known as 'taking the rough with the smooth'.) It has its place, and it may be inescapable within any one bus or train journey, but it leads to serious distortions if it means that outright loss-making mileage has to be provided for by charging more than the traffic will bear in other places. It raises a further problem in that the more profitable parts of a bus company's business will usually lie in the poorer parts of its area, leading to a 'reverse transfer payment', in which people with lower incomes subsidize the better-off. It was applied to the railways in the late 19th century, when the companies were expected by Parliament to build rural branch lines, may of which lost money, and the consequence was to weaken the market position of the railway industry. (It also led in due course to the need for closures, with much public opposition, as the bus and the car made these lines even more of a financial burden.)

CROSS-SUBSIDY, GOOD OR BAD

All selling contains an element of cross-subsidy. The shopkeeper does not expect the same return on every item in the store. In the same way the provision of transport services will often mean that the load carried, whether passengers or parcels, will vary along the route. A bus will leave town with a full load, but there may be only two passengers left at the outer terminal. Much the same can apply where physical distribution is concerned, while loads on trains vary as the journey proceeds. Prices cannot be adjusted to allow for this, and what matters is that the journey or journeys concerned earn sufficient to cover their escapable costs (see Chapter 2). Negative cross-subsidy can occur, though, and it was encouraged within the railway and bus industries for many years. This happens when operation continues when revenue is less than escapable cost, which means that overpricing is required to fund the deficit. To extract this margin it is necessary to have some kind of monopoly, or new competitors will enter the market to undercut the inflated prices. Economists, who agree that the general practice of cross-subsidy is necessary and beneficial, condemn the latter kind, which requires a serious distortion of the market process.

The second system has been described as 'transparent subsidy', because it should be possible to see what benefit will follow from the use of public money to make up any shortfall in revenue. It has been used to keep open a railway line when the revenue that it generates is less than the costs involved (each of these being difficult to calculate). Local authorities adopt it to provide 'socially necessary' bus or train services, and it is assumed that administrators can assess the price that they would be prepared to pay for the provision of such operations. The problem that this raises in economics is the extent to which the market process is distorted, giving rise to costs that are difficult to calculate. Meanwhile costs arise from the administrative system itself. There is also the likelihood that councillors will put pressure on the administrators for such services to be provided in their own wards, seeking to attract votes at the next election, while a branch of economics called public choice theory draws attention to the interest that the administrators themselves have in taking on the job.

These problems become even more severe in the use of the third system, which we may call 'global subsidy'. Here a bus or train operator is told that there is an agreed payment available from public funds to make up for the shortfall of revenue from its customers, so as to provide the network that local or national government desires. A special case of global subsidy is the provision of reduced prices for the elderly and those disabled in any way. This is often seen to be preferable to paying subsidy direct to the operator, but the need for it is called in question by the practice of the railways in Britain of offering cut rates to students, family parties and 'senior citizens' as a marketing exercise. The extreme case of global subsidy is the notion of 'fares free' travel, where there is total subsidy and no pricing at all. A little thought will show that the implications of this for patterns of settlement and commuting could lead to severe problems, but the real criticism lies in the lack of any way of measuring the return that should be obtained from the capital assets concerned.

The foregoing examples apply to passenger movement, and there has never seemed to be very much need for subsidy for the movement of goods. The practice of indirect subsidy has developed in recent years, with public money allocated for the provision of rail sidings for industrial customers, and the improvement of rail and road access to seaports. This aspect of subsidy, however, is complicated by the way in which the infrastructure of the industry – roads and 'rail roads', sea and air ports – is provided, a subject to which we shall return in Chapter 8.

PRICE CONTROL AND THE MARKET

The economic problem behind all provision of subsidy lies in the extent to which it complicates the pricing of transport, since it makes it ever more difficult to identify the costs involved in the movement industry. To interfere with the freedom of managers in any business to choose the prices that they charge is to weaken the very function of management at its heart, and to extend this to the actual control of prices by a public authority, which has no incentive to maximize efficiency, is to distort the catallaxy still more.

We have already seen the consequences of price control for the railway and bus industries, which we can compare with the prosperity of road freight transport and distribution and the financial success of the privately owned rail freight companies. All regulation, as we shall see in the next chapter, tends to reduce economic efficiency, but regulation of fares and charges is a special case. Are there, then, any circumstances in which it may be justified?

Any firm that finds it has a monopoly in its sector of the market will seek to exploit its advantage by raising its prices well above the standard commercial levels, which may be defined as obtaining a return on the firm's capital sufficient to satisfy its opportunity cost (see Chapter 1), together with sufficient margin above that to attract entrepreneurs and to provide funds for further investment. Price control has been used in the past to restrict monopoly power, but it is recognized today that much depends upon the true extent of such power. It used to be argued that certain industries – electricity and gas supply and telephones, for example – were natural monopolies, which therefore required not only price control but also public ownership. Developments in technology have made telecommunications a highly competitive industry, with no need for price control, while for electricity and gas distribution 'grids' have enabled competition to be introduced, subject to the powers of a regulator, and price control is no longer seen to be necessary. Transport has no monopolistic tendency anyway, so in general terms price control cannot be justified.

It is important to define the market in which the firm is active, and the disastrous consequences of price control for the railway and bus industries arose from the failure to recognize that the market is for movement. Even when the railway companies in the 19th century had a strong position in this sense, they were still in competition with road transport, while the private car is inescapably in competition with bus and coach companies. (The former route licensing system for bus and coach services actually created a limited monopoly, which then necessitated price control.) Using the monopoly test, perhaps three main arguments for the retention of price control of transport firms are effective today.

First is the use of superior financial resources to drive out smaller competitors by way of predatory pricing. It is a temptation for a large firm to defend itself in this way, by undercutting the competitor's prices, knowing that any losses incurred can be made up for by raising prices again after the nuisance has gone, and that way the consumer suffers twice over. In the United States it is possible to go to the courts for 'exemplary damages' against the predator (usually three times the loss incurred by the smaller firm), which discourages the practice. In Britain it is the responsibility of the Office of Fair Trading (OFT) to prevent the practice, with the powers of the Monopolies and Mergers Commission in the background. (It must be said that the OFT has found the practice very difficult to regulate.)

Second is the potential for a cartel to appear. A cartel is formed by agreement between a number of firms designed so as to prevent competition between its members, and to stave off entry by newcomers as well. It may extend beyond prices to govern standards of quality and to restrict on-street competition between members of the cartel. Price-fixing of this kind is another problem for the OFT to deal with, but problems have arisen because too strict a regime can prevent joint operation by two or more firms on a given route.

Competition law in this area, in Britain, is directed to maintaining price and quality competition where it is threatened. Outright price control is a different matter, and perhaps the one area in which it is justified is where an element of monopoly does exist, in which one party has a stronger position than the other. The classic example is the taxi trade, where cab drivers pick up passengers on the street or on a rank. (For hire cars it is at least possible to telephone several firms and obtain the best rate that is on offer.) The taxi driver is in a semi-monopolist position, and in the absence of regulation can drive up the price until the customer refuses to pay – but in many cases, especially late at night or in bad weather, the customer may have to accept whatever price is asked, or get no ride. Provided there is no barrier to entry to the trade (as we shall see in the next chapter), price control of this kind probably improves the working of the market, and tends to greater economic efficiency.

CONCLUSION

Irrespective of any other constraints, any market in which prices are 'rigged' is seriously imperfect. It makes no difference whether the rigging is attempted by firms within the market, or imposed by government from without, and while the road and rail freight transport industry has its problems, its freedom from price control plays a great part in its financial success and in satisfying its customers. The growth of low-cost firms in civil aviation shows what can happen when management not only understands costing but is also free to pitch the mix of price and quality where consumer demand prefers it to be.

But as we said at the start of this chapter, there is nothing in economic theory that can enable the 'right' price (or mix of price and quality) for any commodity to be calculated and laid down in advance; neither by managers nor, above all, by regulators. Where monopoly power exists price control may be justified, but as we have seen with the gas and electricity industries, it is better to encourage competition. Too much damage has been done in the past to the railways and to the bus industry by neglect of these principles.

Questions for discussion

1. What are the implications of subsidy for economic efficiency?
2. How can pricing policy attract more business?
3. When may price regulation be justified?

4

Allocative efficiency

WHAT WE SEEK TO ACHIEVE

When something is not scarce (or does not appear to be so), it has no price in exchange, and so it is not the concern of economics. Broadly speaking, the greater the scarcity of any commodity, the higher the price that it will fetch in the market (though fashion may raise the price of quite commonplace things). But in the process of bringing commodities (whether goods or services) to the market, the factors of production (land, labour and capital – see Chapter 1) are used, and insofar as they are scarce, a function of the catallaxy is to tend to achieve their optimal allocation to various uses.

This means that, where there is a fully functioning market, the interplay of supply and demand, through prices that satisfy both producer and consumer (at a given level of quality), provides a constantly changing message for future purposes, reflecting what it is that consumers, in general, want and are willing to pay for. (This is what we call effective demand.) The outcome, in such a situation, is that scarce resources are allocated for various purposes, not by some all-knowing planner, but in the way people have shown that they prefer. This we might call the optimal allocation. At the same time there will be no waste of the kind that must arise where resources are used for purposes that are not justified by the processes of the market. The whole thing shows where economics gets its name from: it is about economizing.

The situation in which supply and demand are in balance, through the working of the price mechanism, is called equilibrium, and this is said to lead to market clearing, where everything that comes to the market is sold, and there is thus no waste. But in real life such a state of affairs, even if it existed for a moment, could never be maintained, because the circumstances of supply and demand, and choices of price and quality on offer, are changing all the time. In other words, while it helps to understand the catallaxy to imagine a state of equilibrium, with the optimal use of scarce resources and the ideal satisfaction of effective demand, the most that we can say is that the market process will constantly tend to such an ideal state of affairs. Matching supply and demand is a pursuit that takes the attention of management all the time, and because the operation of transport at less than capacity is wasteful it is as well that the profit motive exists.

What this is about is called 'efficiency' in economics, a word which, as we saw in Chapter 1, does not have quite the same meaning as it has in engineering. We might refer to it as 'allocative efficiency', and it is hard to see how any other system of allocation could lead to a more satisfactory use of scarce resources. The fact that it must also tend to effectiveness (the satisfaction of effective demand) is something we shall return to in the next chapter, but the two tendencies are inescapably linked.

The factors of production are of course the scarce resources whose use we seek to optimize. (See Chapter 1.) For transport purposes land is of fundamental importance, and in Chapter 8 we shall examine the implications of its scarcity, which is an inescapable problem, and one that has been allowed to distort the allocative process for far too long. Labour, which includes both physical and mental work, presents us with problems, because transport is labour intensive: it is not unusual for the labour cost of a transport business to amount to 60 per cent of the total. Capital, in the sense of wealth available for investment, requires remuneration (which is not the same thing as profit) and as we saw in Chapter 1, if it could have earned more in some other use, there is an opportunity cost. There was a period in the 1950s when much capital was mistakenly invested in the railways, which was wasteful in this way. In each case the market, when it is functioning freely, will tend to an optimum allocation of each of these scarce resources, although the process is always going to be slower for land and capital than it will be for labour.

WHAT PREVENTS PROGRESS

Our understanding of the working of the market, or catallaxy, goes back to the work of Adam Smith, the 18th century founder of what came to be called 'political economy'. Although we rarely observe the working of an unhindered market, the principle remains true that the way people pursue their own satisfactions will, through the multitude of buy/not-buy decisions, tend to the achievement of efficiency and effectiveness, in the absence of external constraints. In the 20th century Friedrich Hayek stressed the importance of spontaneity in the market; the catallaxy is a process that could never have been invented or planned. 'To err is human', so we cannot expect the process always to be fault-free, and so there is always the possibility of market failure, but this in no way weakens the argument for a free and open market as the best assurance we can have that efficiency and effectiveness are being pursued.

Before anything else, the catallaxy depends upon the contestability of the market, which is the level of ease of both entry and exit. In a perfectly contestable market there will be no barriers, and firms may engage in hit-and-run competition, to an extent that is made more difficult by the existence of economies of scale. To the extent that they do so, they will keep the more established firms on their toes. For obvious reasons hit-and-run competition is unpopular with the establishment, but that it can tend to the advantage of consumers cannot be doubted. It is common in trades like window cleaning, although even there an informal agreement usually exists whereby each individual defends his or her own territory. Similar territorial agreements have existed for many years in the bus industry (see the box and Chapter 10), but for transport in general the principal barrier to entry is quantity regulation (see below).

PIRATE BUSES IN LONDON

The horse bus industry in London, which originated with Shillibeer's Omnibus in 1829, was organized in a series of route associations. Each was a form of cartel whose members agreed the frequency and fares. From time to time a new operator, a 'pirate', would appear on the route and the Association would respond by 'nursing' the newcomer. Buses would be designated to run just before the newcomer, so as to take up the passengers waiting at the stops. If the pirate survived, the operator would be invited to join the Association, and to take part in future nursing exercises.

The importance of ease of exit for the degree of contestability is linked to the problem of sunk cost, which we examined in Chapter 1. Where the assets of a firm, such as underground rail tunnels in cities, have no alternative use, the only available exit is through bankruptcy, and any risk of being caught with unsaleable investments will discourage newcomers from the sector of the market concerned. The case for separate ownership of railway track and train operation has been seen to turn upon this since the early days of the industry, and if steam traction had been applied to roads instead of rails in the 1830s the problems of the transport industry would be quite different today. Heavy investment thresholds, however, have not prevented low-cost airlines from showing that civil aviation is a more contestable industry than had previously been assumed.

An example of human error is the way in which business managers try to avoid competition. The economist Joan Robinson remarked that 'the greatest monopoly profit is a quiet life', reflecting that the competitive process is demanding, so company directors and managers may not always fit the commonly held stereotype of profit maximization; though in fact it is desirable that they should. There is also the constant (though short-sighted) temptation of 'rigging the market', which we saw in Chapter 3, so as to achieve price fixing or the development of a cartel. Where the market is highly competitive, as in the case of freight transport and distribution, such practices are hard to maintain, and quickly break down, but the passenger transport industry has always been given to them. This is because of the relative weakness of the consumer; the individual passenger has little bargaining power where bus or train services are concerned, compared with the customer of a road haulage firm.

THE STRANGE DECLINE OF THE BRITISH BUS INDUSTRY

After 1916 the big combines that were becoming increasingly dominant in the provision of bus services in Britain sought to see to it that their subsidiary companies did not compete with each other. The 'area agreements' that they designed were almost certainly impossible to defend at law, being 'contracts in restraint of trade', but they left each party free to compete with smaller firms within its territory, and it was in no one's interest to test their defensibility. This was a kind of cartel, an example of market failure, but when it was strengthened by the route licensing system introduced in 1930 it came to be also a regulatory failure. As a result of this, managers, thinking they had taken care of the competition, failed to recognize that after 1950 a new competitor – the private car – had appeared in the market, and they took no steps to respond to it. It seems strange to remember that the introduction of route monopolies was supposedly justified on the grounds that competition produced 'wasteful duplication'.

Market failure of this kind may be controlled by legislation that makes it an offence to indulge in restrictive practices. We have seen in Chapter 3 the difficulties that arise when this is applied to the way fares and charges are arrived at, but there is a much wider area within which regulation may be, and commonly is, a constraint upon the efficiency of the transport industry. Introduced with the best of intentions, controls of this kind all too often lead to regulatory failure, which is capable of distorting the catallaxy and inhibiting the allocative efficiency of the industry at least as much as the incidence of market failure. The outcome is an increased burden on the taxpayer, for the cost of failure does not fall upon the individual administrators. We shall return to this subject in Chapter 5.

THE CONSEQUENCES OF REGULATION

Transport is a fail-dangerous industry; mechanical or operational failure is always more likely to cause injury and even death than the activities of manufacturing or the retail trade. It may also be described as opaque, which means that it is normally impossible even for a qualified engineer to be satisfied that a bus or train is safe to board. Trusting in a transport firm's reputation may not be enough to provide peace of mind, although it plays a large part in the choice of contractor for the movement of goods and for distribution; but you do not get any choice at the railway station or the bus stop, or when hailing a taxi.

Unscrupulous firms may seek to cut corners by failing to maintain their vehicles in a safe condition, or recruiting operating and engineering staff who are not well trained for their jobs, or who are simply unreliable. They may also fail to maintain proper records, or even to know where the danger points are. (This is a special problem with the provision of the transport infrastructure, which we shall discuss in Chapter 8.) In a theoretically fully open or contestable market the opportunity for 'hit-and-run' competition must make safety a serious risk. This is why safety regulation, sometimes called quality control, is necessary for all forms of transport, and this has been recognized since the early days of railways.

While we might expect to find that in any business there is good reason to maintain the equipment in safe working order, and to employ adequately trained staff, the risk of firms taking short cuts, not least when faced with financial problems, means that intervention is needed. This is to protect three classes of people: passengers (in the passenger carrying business), operating staff, and third parties. In the case of freight transport it is for the shipper to assess the risk of loss or damage to goods, but danger to staff and third parties (anyone who may become involved in an accident, for example) applies to all modes of transport, including its infrastructure. Each aspect interacts with the others, so that quality control is a wide-ranging activity of government, and of the insurance industry. It must be recognized to be a constraint on the working of the market, but so long as it is reasonably designed and administered it is a necessity that must be allowed for.

The problem is that, as with all forms of intervention, quality control is open to regulatory failure. As we shall see in Chapter 5, those who design and administer it have a vested interest in making it ever more extensive and complex, since it is the source of their employment and reward, and every serious accident leads to calls from politicians and the public for 'absolute safety'. While this is a state of affairs that can never be achieved, a result may be still more complex and sometimes contradictory regulation, and further intervention in the working of the market. What sounds like a straightforward solution to a genuine problem can and does become a growing constraint upon the allocative efficiency of the industry. It can also inhibit innovation, either because of over-caution or through sheer inefficiency of the regulatory authority.

Privatization of the railways should have been designed to restore the industry to 'the discipline of the market', but the outcome was a disappointment, as we shall see in Chapter 11. So much power to intervene was given to the administrators that the interests of the passengers seemed to get lost in the structure. It would seem that the government was frightened to go so far as to have a railway system regulated only for safety, and the outcome was a series of compromises that have led eventually to the return of the railways to state control. But failure in practice does not have to imply that the original argument from economics was wrong.

RAILTRACK AND REGULATORY FAILURE

The history of Railtrack plc was marked by controversy, but some study of its design and function shows how intervention can have unintended, expensive and indeed disastrous consequences. Originally set up as a public authority under a 'light touch' regulator, it was sold by HM Treasury into the private sector without a strengthening of the regulatory powers. But Railtrack was also intended to be a regulator itself, both in supervising its contractors and in approving the design and performance of new rolling stock for the train operating companies and the rail freight business. Its failure in the first example led to more, not less danger, while its ineffective and tardy processes led to wasted investment in the movement side of the railway, and still further inefficiency. Then the policy of the regulator to force down the track access charges paid by the train operators was a form of price control that went wrong, since it reduced the amount of money available for investment in the track itself.

One problem with all forms of regulation is the need for some form of enforcement. The most effective system is to require firms or individuals to hold a certificate or licence. If a firm is shown to have failed to maintain the requisite standards, the licence can be suspended or cancelled, with the consequence that the firm can no longer trade. The EU Operator's Licence (see Chapter 9) is designed with this in mind, and in the United Kingdom operators can be called before the Licensing Authority, which has powers to enforce quality regulation in this way. The regulations concern both mechanical safety and operational procedures, and impose a complex set of rules concerning the number of hours that drivers are permitted to work, either at the wheel or in other activities.

Safety regulations apply to licensed taxicabs and to hire cars, but with no limitations on hours of driving. The extension of quality control to the use of private cars for business purposes (or even for private use) would be highly controversial, and the so-called 'MOT

Test', which is very limited when compared to the requirement for some (but not all) commercial vehicles, does not place any limit on hours spent driving. Yet though there have been many serious accidents caused by the car driver's tiredness, the problem facing those who would extend regulation turns upon the difficulty of enforcing it. (The use of mobile phones while driving is an example of the same problem.)

The economic problems associated with regulation become more serious yet when they extend to the imposition of quantity control, which confers monopoly rights upon the fortunate licence holder. This is extremely difficult to justify, and in recent years many examples of this kind of intervention have been repealed or abandoned. At one time many city councils limited the number of taxicab licences that they would issue, providing a form of monopoly, and when the restriction was removed (leaving only quality control in place) there were strong protests on the part of cab drivers, who would probably have preferred to see such limits applied to the hire car business.

We have already noted (see the box on page 33) the consequences of route licensing for the bus and coach industry, which was introduced after representations to a Royal Commission on Transport by the area agreement and municipal operators, who wanted protection from smaller competitors. (It was drastically reduced by the deregulation act of 1985.) It is hard to avoid the conclusion that quantity control acts to the disadvantage of the consumer, by protecting those who hold the licence from competition. The outcome in terms of allocative efficiency hardly needs to be emphasized.

The remaining example of this kind of intervention in the market process is the imposition of price control, which we examined in Chapter 3. As we have seen, it may be justified where an element of monopoly exists, but in any other circumstances it has the most serious consequences of any type of regulation, in that it limits the freedom of management at the heart of the economic process: setting prices in a competitive market. We shall return to the problem in Chapter 10.

PUBLIC OWNERSHIP AND FRANCHISE AS REGULATION

One way of looking at the nationalization of railways in Britain in 1947 is to see it as a final step in Parliament's attempts to arrive at an effective system of regulation. In the light of economics there is an element of irony when we see rail transport still being treated as a monopoly, whereas it has been competing in the market for movement throughout its history, and increasingly so since the 1950s. It rapidly became plain that the British Transport Commission was unable to second-guess the market, and to plan for the efficient allocation of scarce resources, either from its railways or from any other of its responsibilities. Recognition of this led in due course to the reprivatization of the state-owned transport businesses progressively after 1962.

Another way is to see state or public ownership as the extreme form of intervention in the market; as if there could be a disinterested public authority which knew best how to arrive at efficiency. The idea of the catallaxy is forgotten here, being replaced by economic planning, with objectives that are hard to define and in practice unattainable, because of the uncertainties of the future. The power of the consumer is also negated, as we shall see in the next chapter, since the all-knowing authority is assumed to 'know best what is good for the punters'. The element of risk inherent in all investment, given the unknown future, presents a problem, since administrators, dealing with public funds, must always be risk-averse. This means also that innovation will be discouraged, while the standardization of management leaves little opportunity for people with original ideas to progress. One of the virtues of the open or contestable market is that there is always a call for new thinking, challenging the conventional wisdom, as well as for new capital which is seeking the opportunities that may follow from the new ideas.

State ownership can take several forms. In some countries, public transport is a direct function of the state, and the responsibility of a department of government. The British model, sometimes called 'arm's length' nationalization, places ownership and management under the control of a board appointed by the government department concerned, with objectives that have generally been unclear. Such a board is not the same as a board of directors with a financial responsibility to its shareholders; while, unlike company directors, board members seldom suffer from the consequences of their mistakes. Public ownership by elected local authorities has sometimes involved delegating control to a manager on an arm's length basis, but always there is the interest of the elected representatives in achieving success at the polls. Many of the achievements of local authority transport managers in the past date from the period before the provision of public transport was faced with the competition of the private car.

More recently the inherent problems of public ownership have led local authorities in many parts of the world to explore the greater cost-effectiveness of private enterprise. This is a compromise solution, whereby the provision of transport services is said to be franchised, with routes, frequencies, fares and even the type of vehicle still to be controlled by the authority. Companies are invited to tender for the privilege of profitable operation of the franchise over a period of years, after which it will be re-tendered. This is a specialized form of arm's length public ownership, designed to exploit the lower costs of the private sector operator while retaining control of the market (insofar as that is ever possible). It must not be confused with the 'ethical franchise' which is to be found in many parts of the retail trade and service industries, where the franchisee is in a very different situation.

The economist must be aware of the serious misunderstanding that is commonly to be found where the use of franchise is discussed. Proponents of the system argue that it is a form of market competition, using the term 'competing for the market' instead of 'competing in the market'. This makes no sense in economics, for the tendering companies are in fact competing for a monopoly, even though it may be controlled by a 'competent authority'. There is no way in which such franchises can be shown to tend to allocative efficiency, any more than is possible with any system that involves intervention in the market.

PEOPLE IN BUSINESS

Economists sometimes use the term 'rent' to refer to financial returns received by the firm over and above those that should cover the opportunity cost of the resources that it owns. Profit arising from successful innovation is an example of rent, and this leads the firm to shift scarce resources into more highly valued uses, and so tends to optimize allocation in the economy. But rent-seeking has another and less beneficial outcome, which arises when individuals within the firm seek economic advantages for themselves. In Chapter 5 we shall examine the insights of public choice theory in the administrative and political world, and its implications for the satisfaction of the consumer, but while officials and politicians cannot be assumed to be free of self-interest, neither can people involved in private industry. The consequences may be less distortive among sole traders and small firms, where the realities of the marketplace are more obvious to the eye, but they can become a serious constraint upon economic efficiency if they are not corrected within the larger firm.

Rent-seeking can be found at every level in a business organization. While the theory of the firm assumes that all pressure will be upon achieving a satisfactory return from the assets, together with profits arising from innovation and constructive marketing, there is as we have seen a preference for a quiet life as against the effort needed to succeed in the market. This may lead to cartels and agreements not to compete, which have always been prevalent in merchant shipping, as well as in the bus industry. That is an example of rent-seeking at board and executive level, and it leads serious distortions in allocative efficiency. But within the business organization rent-seeking may be found in a range of attitudes and activities, in which managers seek to make personal gains which conflict with the better interests of the firm, and thus of the economy. There can be quite a fine distinction between legitimate pursuit of promotion on the one hand, and the temptation for managers to improve their pay and status in ways that conflict, to a greater or less extent, with the best interest of the company. Various departments can become in effect autonomous, and this may lead to their pursuit of objectives that are actually counterproductive, and opposed to those found in other parts of the business.

These problems may be seen as diseconomies of large scale, and it is to be hoped that a success-oriented business will avoid them. But they have led to some catastrophic collapses, with severe losses experienced by shareholders, employees and their families, and which weaken the working of the catallaxy with its hoped-for tendency to optimize the allocation of scarce resources.

A SILLY IDEA

From time to time the media report comments by members of the public, and sometimes by people who should know better, criticizing transport for, it is claimed, 'putting profits before the interest of the customer'. The short answer to this is that the firm that fails to make profits will go out of business, and if the industry at large is losing money it will attract subsidy from the public purse, at the taxpayer's expense, and this will increase the power of administrators and politicians, which, as public choice theory shows (see Chapter 5), always tends to introduce regulatory failure, which makes things worse. Part of the problem here is the popular misunderstanding of the word 'profit', which is a bit more complicated than most people seem to assume.

The first objective of the firm must be to maintain its assets in good condition; to replace them as necessary; and at every stage to be satisfied that their financial contribution is such as to justify keeping them in the same operation, or alternatively, finding an operation that increases the return. If they fail, there is an opportunity cost; any shortfall between what they are earning and what they might earn in another use is a cost to the business. So long as the firm is broadly pursuing such a policy it will tend to increase allocative efficiency, which we have seen to be a highly desirable outcome. But the uncertainty of the future, and the hope for reward over and above the return on assets, introduces the entrepreneur (see Chapter 5), one of whose functions is innovation, without which the customer will soon have cause for complaint. But innovation means risk, and that is what, if the innovation is successful, must be rewarded with profits. If it fails, there will be a loss.

It is true that the process outlined here is subject to market failure, but, as we saw in Chapter 1, it is hard to find any alternative that would be likely to improve on it, in its dual function of satisfying the customer and tending to improve allocative efficiency. In Part Three we shall be looking at the importance of marketing in the process, and it may be a legitimate criticism of the passenger transport industry that it does not have a record of great success in that area. It is, however, interesting to see that the 'profits before customers' complaint is seldom heard from customers in the highly competitive freight transport industry, perhaps because the customers are other businesses.

IS THERE SOMETHING SPECIAL ABOUT TRANSPORT?

Politicians, journalists and commentators on transport matters, perhaps reflecting public opinion, frequently assume that the normal objectives of business do not apply to the movement industries. The failure of Railtrack plc (see the box on page 36) led to calls for the renationalization of railways (which has now in effect taken place), despite the failure of the state-owned system to attract sufficient investment from government over the period since 1947; a failure inevitable so long as the railways have to compete with education and health for the limited availability of public funds. Local authorities have been allowed to invest public money in tramcar systems without the constraint of the opportunity cost rules laid down by HM Treasury in the 1960s, or the similar general constraints that exist in the private sector. The discussion of allocatory efficiency or opportunity cost is seldom heard in the arguments for and against public ownership in transport.

Public ownership, as we have seen, is the ultimate example of intervention in the market, and its outcome is invariably to place constraints upon the market process, and so to reduce the efficiency of the industry concerned. As we shall see in the next chapter, the effective demand of the consumer loses out to the well-intentioned intervention of the administrator, whose motives are coloured by vested interest, and affected by the desire of elected representatives to maximize votes at the next election. The economist must always be alert to the implications of intervention of this kind, and will be suspicious of any argument that seeks to limit the beneficial processes of the market. People who have used public transport in France, Germany or Switzerland see the quality of the system, but do not realize the amount of public money spent on it, or question whether or not it was wisely spent.

The idea that transport is essential and therefore not like other business is commonly to be heard in the European Union, where franchise is seen in some states to be an acceptable alternative to competition. The same idea is to be heard in Britain, especially where railway transport is concerned. (Perhaps the railways attract an emotional response from people who played with train sets when they were children.) But the consequences of such an attitude in many European states, in some of which subsidy runs at 80 per cent (see Table 4.1), are now becoming plain, in the distortions that follow when opportunity cost is neglected or ignored. Ultimately, it is only in the catallaxy that there will be a reliable tendency for allocative efficiency to be maximized.

It is strange to see how people seem to think that transport is something special, which they fail to understand, and nowhere is this more true than in attitudes to the private car (which we shall examine in Chapter 7). Another aspect of this is the way in which so many enthusiasts seem unwilling to master the policy issues and constraints that encircle the industry; and above all, there is the nostalgia that prevents people from recognizing that the past may not always be relevant for the industry today.

All the same, it is hard to escape the conclusion that there is something special about transport. Many people in all walks of life seek satisfactions from their work in addition to the wages or salary provided for in their contract of employment. Some of these may be described as non-monetary satisfactions, many of which people derive from working in a transport business, such is the attraction of the industry for those involved in it, whether in railways, ships, buses, aircraft or whatever. The labour market is affected by this in two ways.

Table 4.1 Proportion of operating costs financed from fares and subsidies

City	% from public subsidy and grants	% from fares and other commercial sources
Dublin	4	96
Lisbon	27	73
Manchester	34	66
Copenhagen	34	66
Barcelona	35	65
Athens	45	55
Cologne *	45	55
Lyons *	51	49
Helsinki *	51	49
Stockholm *	52	48
Rotterdam *	68	32
Antwerp *	69	31
Turin *	70	30
Vienna	70	30
Luxembourg	75	25

Note: * In these cities the figures include tram, metro or light rail. The remainder are bus only. Data relates to the late 1990s. Subsidy for Greater Manchester listed above comes from the following sources: reimbursement of concessionary fares, fuel duty rebate and financially supported mileage.

Source: Confederation of Passenger Transport UK, *Facts 2002*. While high standards of public transport are capable of being provided with substantial subsidy, the consequent burden of taxation as well as the problems of opportunity cost are leading governments to review the justification for such policies.

One is the contribution to management and operation of valuable insights, and what may be called flair, which can contribute to the success of the firm, and so to the satisfaction of effective demand, while the obverse of this arises from evidence that posts in transport management may offer lower financial reward than equivalent positions in industry in general. Readers of this book who are contemplating a career in transport because of their understanding of one or another mode may like to reflect upon what they have to offer in this way.

CONCLUSION

Adam Smith likened the processes of the market to an 'invisible hand', more efficient than any central organization in the coordination of wants and supplies. People produce goods and services to meet the needs of other people whom they may never meet, and for whom they feel no goodwill; while we satisfy our own wants from the produce of others whom we do not need to know. This, the catallaxy, is subject to its own weaknesses: monopoly, external costs and benefits, and uneven distribution of income, each of which we shall discuss in turn, and it is open to the inefficiencies that follow from intervention, however well intentioned. Too often the results of regulatory failure are mistakenly assumed to be failures in the transport market itself,

It is the function of the invisible hand to tend to the achievement of two objectives: efficiency, as we have discussed it here, and effectiveness, which as we have seen is the satisfaction of the effective demand of consumers in the market. The two processes are inextricably linked, and they may not always go forward at the same rate. Innovation and technical progress may be delayed in reaching the market because of necessary quality control, or through the working of the market for capital. In the next chapter we shall be looking at the subjects we have just discussed from the point of view of the customer.

Questions for discussion

1. What is meant by market failure?
2. What causes regulatory failure?
3. How best can transport firms respond to demand?

5

Consumer effectiveness

SATISFYING EFFECTIVE DEMAND

We have now seen how the market process, the catallaxy, whatever failures there may be that constrain it, will tend to the optimum allocation of scarce resources; that is to say, to economic efficiency. Out of the unmeasurable number of buy/not-buy decisions in the market, signals are sent around that affect the make/not-make decisions of suppliers of all kinds of goods and services. And as we have seen, this process has evolved naturally, and has succeeded because it gives satisfaction to those involved in it. But however satisfying it is to know that the factors of production are employed in such a way, it is equally important for us to stress the effectiveness of the process, in terms of providing what people want, and are prepared to pay for, at the levels of price and quality that they, and they alone, can judge to be satisfactory.

If we turn to the supply of consumer goods (food, clothes, groceries, furniture and so on) we can see how competitive pressure tends to keep prices down and push quality up, putting the consumer's interests, on balance, before the short-term interests of industry. Firms in the retail trade that ignore this (and several names will come to mind) find their profits falling, along with the value of their shares in the market. We can see also how the market encourages a range of suppliers and retailers, offering various mixes of price and quality, which caters for the range of tastes and spending power to be found in human society. Attempts to replace this arrangement in states that have sought to achieve a controlled economy have always failed (as they must), and have always given rise to a 'black economy', favouring those who can afford to pay for choice. And the market process goes further, in allowing for changes in public taste to make themselves felt, provided there is room for those in business to try and forecast the future, and risk their money in seeking to take advantage from potential changes in price, quality and taste. These people are called entrepreneurs.

THE IMPORTANCE OF THE ENTREPRENEUR

We have already seen that a static economy is an impossible concept, and that the future must always be a matter of greater or less uncertainty. The entrepreneur will, for purely selfish reasons, bring changes about that may turn out to be profitable; and whether they are or not, they will tend to improve the efficiency of the market process, and also to increase the effective satisfaction of individuals' demands. But the entrepreneur has a disturbing function, and tends to be suspect in the eyes of those who like to see things going on as they always have done in the past.

There are three types of entrepreneur, the arbitrageur, the speculator and the innovator. It is important to remember that, since the future is full of uncertainty, their attempts to 'second-guess' the course of events in order to make profits are subject to risk; if they get it wrong, they stand to lose. And because uncertainty follows upon uncertainty, the further forward you try to forecast the future, the more likely you are to get it wrong. Arbitrageurs and speculators seek to make money by spotting weaknesses in the relationship between prices or between costs in various parts of the market. Thus the former may buy in one place, where prices are low, so as to make a profit by reselling elsewhere, where the going price is higher. This will tend to bring prices into line with each other, and so to improve the working of the market, which will tend to equilibrium. Speculators seek to do the same, but for them it is potential imbalance that they foresee or forecast, as where a dealer builds up a stock of some commodity that might be expected to be affected by changes in taste, and thus might come to be in short supply for a time. While we may feel an understandable jealousy when these people get it right, and seem to be taking an unfair advantage, they are of course quite likely to get their calculations wrong, and lose rather than gain in the process, while here again they tend to improve the working of the market.

Arbitrageurs and speculators make their profits from situations over which they have no control, whereas innovators hope to bring profitable changes into effect by their own action. That is no doubt why we think more highly of the innovator, but it remains true that the new invention that is being financed at risk could be a failure. Hundreds of inventions are registered at the Patent Office each year, and the great majority of them will offer no likely contribution to the increase of human happiness. Most of them will not be taken up by an entrepreneur, but of those that are then financed and developed to be placed on the market, there is every possibility that many will not attract sufficient demand to repay the investment required.

Innovation is the key to progress and the origin of all improvements in the qualities and prices of goods and services on offer, but innovators, along with speculators, have a disequilibriating effect in the market. There is a tendency to inertia in the productive process; just as we have seen that 'the greatest monopoly profit is a quiet life', so it is always tempting to go on selling the same product at whatever price the market will accept. The innovator is thus a disturbing influence, and may not be welcome. It is always possible that business executives will try to forestall the problem, by rigging the market in various ways. As customers we may not always welcome the changes that follow from such profit-seeking activities, since we so easily become set in our ways, but ultimately it is innovation that weights the market process in favour of the consumer.

Innovation has an important function in encouraging cheapening. As we have seen, a given item will be cheaper if its quality improves while its price remains the same, but sometimes the standards of quality may be higher than an open market would justify. Thus the low cost 'no-frills' airlines have shown that the consumer is, up to a point, more concerned about price than quality, provided safety standards are assured. So long as the civil aviation market was subject to quantity control, such an adaptation was impossible, but when it came it was the consequence of speculative innovation that challenged the assumptions of airline managers in the larger firms, who had clearly failed to assess the market for flying. And after all, it might not have worked.

One problem for the innovator in any service industry, such as transport, is that there is little you can do about it if your forecasts do fail. As we saw in Chapter 1, the product of a service industry is instantaneously perishable (we shall return to this problem in Part Three). So the risk involved in all innovation is enhanced by the fact that there is nothing you can do about it if you got your forecast wrong. Many a new bus service has had to be withdrawn after a few months' operation, because people did not want it enough to use it, so that the output in terms of seat-miles contained an element of money 'running to waste'. Though we may learn from our mistakes, it still costs money to make them, when the output concerned cannot be stored. The satisfaction of effective demand is not as simple as it might seem, but the signals that come from the market can indicate the least risky route, and there is no better way of getting it right.

In a perfect world, were such a thing possible, the processes of the catallaxy would function side by side, to optimize economic efficiency and to maximize the satisfaction of effective demand. In practice the two cannot be relied upon to proceed at the same pace, and in the short run they may function in conflict. We have seen, too, that the pursuit of allocative efficiency by industry cannot be relied upon 100 per cent, and that the satisfaction of consumers' effective demand may not always be a priority within the business. Despite market failures, though, there does not seem to be any better way to achieve effective supply of goods and services than the free working of a contestable market (subject to the requirements of safety control), so it comes as a disappointment to find that the process is all too often disturbed by government itself, and what may be called regulatory failures.

REGULATORY FAILURE AND THE ECONOMICS OF PUBLIC CHOICE

There is a widespread assumption that individuals and firms in business seek only their private gains, and that in consequence they need to be regulated, before they waste natural resources, damage the environment, sell shoddy and dangerous goods and services, place their employees at risk, use misleading advertising and – not least – 'rig the market'. All this is seen to justify intervention by government agencies of various kinds, which purport to be supervised by Parliament. While there is an element of truth in all this, the market today is subject to massive intervention and insidious regulation, which imposes costs on producers, and impedes the process of the catallaxy at every stage.

We have already made the important distinction between quality control on the one hand, which may be justified by the need to ensure safety, as against quantity control, which creates a monopoly that then has to be supervised to prevent its exploitation, and price control, which is justified only where monopoly situations arise (as in the case of taxis plying for hire). We recognize that firms will seek to rig the market, perhaps by establishing cartels or other agreements not to compete, but economic theory tells us that measures to deal with market failure must always be limited to their immediate necessity. Indeed, it is arguable that in the long run, market failures will correct themselves, and any intervention is likely to make the situation worse; but the problem here is the failure in effectiveness during the period of adjustment in terms of efficiency.

It cannot be denied that intervention can easily introduce regulatory failure, although this is not widely recognized. We have already seen that the costs of enforcement form a burden on public funds, but there is also the problem that imperfect enforcement brings the objective into disrepute, as in the example of police cameras intended to enforce speed limits on the highway. What is too little recognized, however, is that we fail to apply the economics of private choice – the decision making of individuals and firms – to the decisions of the public servants who design and administer the regulations, and of the politicians who are ultimately responsible for them.

Individuals and firms in the market certainly seek their private gains; this is what drives the catallaxy. Even so, there are abundant examples of decisions that respect ethical considerations, either in principle or because it is seen to be good for the reputation of the firm. Indeed, pressure from non-government organizations (NGOs) which do not understand the catallaxy and the benefits of free trade can lead to decisions that weaken the market's tendency to allocative efficiency. But in any case, the pursuit of private gains at the expense of the customer can only be self-defeating in due course. The market is untidy, but since Adam Smith first identified it, we have observed the 'hidden hand' which benefits us all, but which comes from self-seeking decisions.

What is strange is that, in contrast to this, it is widely assumed that government intervention in the economy is undertaken by public-spirited public servants seeking only to promote the general welfare. In practice, this is to ignore the fact that the same rational, self-seeking motives that we observe in the market process guide decision making in the public sector as well. Our administrators and our elected representatives do not leave their personal interests at home when they go to the office, to Parliament or to the Town Hall.

Government departments, whether local or national, are 'bureaucratic' organizations, and we often refer to them as bureaucracies. Even large businesses can become bureaucratic in their organization, but when they do they perform badly, and sooner or later (usually sooner) they will either fail or be restructured. In the public sector, where there is no rigorous measure of success or failure, bureaucracies habitually seek to preserve their existence, and indeed to expand it. From time to time this may be checked by wiser administration, or by political pressure, but the fact remains that the bureaucrats have an incentive to preserve their organization, which is often at odds with the pursuit of policies that would benefit consumers in the market. The privatization of various parts of the transport industry has been driven by the principle that the consumer should ultimately decide issues of price and quality, and thus of investment, and not the bureaucrat.

The problem is that public officials are subject to the same temptations that we saw in Chapter 4 when we looked at rent-seeking in business; they want to expand their responsibilities and their departments, giving themselves, and their staff, increased status and higher salaries. The problem is that the costs fall on the tax-payer, who will not be aware of the process as it happens, and who has no effective opportunity to protest until it is too late. Policy decisions defended on the argument that they are for 'the public good' are difficult to criticize, since the public good is generally impossible to measure. (We shall return to this problem when we examine 'externalities' in Chapter 6.) Policies and programmes are developed and presented to the public, often with untestable assumptions, but the fact remains that those responsible for them gain power and status from their design and administration, whether they are desirable or not. Public choice theory, however, seeks to discover, as precisely and carefully as possible, who gains and who loses and by how much. The same rational, self-interest-seeking behaviour that motivates human action in the private sector will be found to apply in the public sector as well. But whereas the market, with all its faults, turns this to the general advantage, regulatory failure shows up in costs which we all bear, yet which we are unable to measure or to resist.

Public officials, of course, are not solely responsible for the policies that they introduce and administer. These decisions rest ultimately with our elected representatives. But as any reader who saw the television series *Yes, Minister* or *Yes, Prime Minister* will understand, the 'Platonic Guardians', as they have been called, play a large part in the design and implementation of public policy, and this is as true at the level of local councils as it is in Westminster. But councillors and Members of Parliament have their own econ-omic agenda, which is to be re-elected: a factor that public choice theory defines as the vote motive.

As a source of intervention and distortion of the market, this influence operates at the level of both central and local government. Ironically, it may be rent-seeking by businesses that leads to pres-sure upon MPs and councillors to introduce and pursue polices that lead in turn to regulatory failure. In extreme cases this may amount to corruption, but just as we have seen that administrators have their own economic agenda, so too do our elected representatives. An MP who seeks promotion into government will obey the whips' instructions, whether he or she agrees with the policy concerned or not. Ministers will deploy 'spin' to influence public opinion, with the aim of retaining their party's control of the House of Commons; not always being over-careful to tell the truth. At local level, councillors may put the short-term interests of their wards before the wider interest of the town or city, so as to improve their chances of being re-elected, while entrenched party control can lead to policy decisions escaping serious criticism or correction. Even governments can make decisions without due thought as to their consequences, which may be difficult to correct. Free travel on rural buses, for example, could lead to the closure of rural shops and post offices. Winston Churchill expressed the problem well, when he suggested that 'democracy is the worst form of government except all those other forms that have been tried from time to time' (speech in the House of Commons, 11 November 1947).

The vote motive and regulatory failure, then, are closely linked. Along with them goes the tendency of certain professions, notably in the legal world, to ban competition among themselves, creating what are in effect cartels. The conclusion from public choice theory must be that, taken together, these practices do not encourage allocative efficiency, but neither do they necessarily lead to the effective satisfaction of consumer demand; rather, their effect is to interfere with the market process that tends to such satisfaction. But the underlying problem lies in the inertia of the legislative and administrative systems, which makes it difficult to correct mistakes or to control the self-seeking attitudes that public choice theory has identified.

FORECASTING DEMAND

It is the function of the entrepreneur to seek to profit by forecasting the future, accepting the risk that must follow if the forecast is wrong, as it often inevitably must be. But success in satisfying effective demand must turn upon the ability to foresee consumer choice. Those who introduced the ball-point pen must have foreseen that people would prefer it to the steel pen and the inkwell, or even to the fountain pen, so that they would rapidly dominate the market for writing instruments, while the sheer scale of demand enabled the unit cost and price of the new product to fall and thus to expand demand still more. Management in the bus industry, on the other hand, failed to foresee that the same process would follow from the mass production of private cars after 1945, until it was almost too late. But unlike the ball-point pen, the private car requires substantial investment in the provision of roads (and garages), which is why the process is so much more problematical for transport.

Day-to-day forecasting can call upon data from existing trends, while market research can explore the need for change. The corporate plan for the business will set out the expected patterns of demand for the products, and the various departments of management will function to apply or to correct these assumptions. But businesses must recognize that the further into the future you seek to plan in this way, the greater is the risk that you will be wrong. And if you are wrong, and you have invested heavily in machinery and other assets, then economics tells us that you must be ready to write off this mistaken investment, and start again from the new situation. The mistaken investment in steam locomotives by British Railways after 1947 is a good example of this.

Major changes in technology, like the invention of the ball-point pen or the vacuum cleaner, are obvious examples of the uncertainty of future demand, while it should be possible to forecast the consequences of changes in production technology, such as the mass production of cars or the rapid expansion of capacity in airliners (whose cheapening effect put an end to the Atlantic passenger shipping trade). What is more difficult to allow for is the inherent uncertainty of the catallactic process. This is made plain by the application of chaos theory, which we shall examine in Chapter 18. In the nature of things, the dynamics of change as we move into the future will be unstable, and the application of what was called 'linear programming' is inherently misleading. The dynamics of change are, for the most part, non-linear, and this must leave the market open for the entrepreneur to understand, but always with the risk of being wrong.

Non-linear dynamics presents us with the situation in which the links between cause and effect are more complex than business planning tends to assume. While broad categories of behaviour, such as we have just seen, can be recognized, small changes in the flow of events can have disproportionate consequences that are impossible to foresee. The competitive market is best able to allow firms to adapt to the mixture of order and disorder that chaos theory identifies, and so long as the proprietor is flexible in changing the strategy in this way, small firms that lie close to the market will be able to handle the situation, while large businesses are at risk if they are tied to rigid forecasting and complex corporate plans.

What is always difficult, though, is to predict and provide for investment on a large scale that requires a period of years before it can be commissioned for use. Ships are a good example, and so are motorways and bridges, and the upgrading of railway facilities. These are problems of sunk cost, where mistaken investment can lead to financial consequences. Shipping companies that place orders for tankers, expecting delivery in three years' time, must face the risk that the market for oil may have collapsed, leading to surplus capacity and falling revenues, but government departments that authorize the building of bridges or motorways that fail to attract the use that was predicted merely pass the consequences on to the taxpayer.

For an effective market, decisions should always tend to improve the satisfaction of effective demand, while tending to economic efficiency. Forecasting the future of effective demand is not going to be easy, but the further ahead you seek to plan, the more such forecasts are likely to be wrong. In this situation the structure of an industry must enable self-transformation, allowing firms to adapt their plans as the catallaxy proceeds. To expect this of public sector authorities, subject as they are to the problems we have seen in public choice theory, is to ask a great deal, but unless their plans and promises take account of non-linear dynamics it will be the consumer, as taxpayer, who will suffer.

CONCLUSION

The customer is always right, we are told, but whereas the working of the market will always tend to empower the consumer, there are always problems along the way. For one thing, market failures that need to be corrected to improve economic efficiency may delay the satisfaction of effective demand, and while the skills of the entrepreneur work to that desirable end, there are many factors in the business world that can interfere. Perhaps the greatest problem, though, is that attempts by public authorities to correct market failures too often make the situation worse, because of the little-recognized phenomenon of regulatory failure, due to the perfectly human self-seeking behaviour that characterizes administrators and elected representatives.

What we have seen in this chapter and the preceding one is the force of the economist's defence of a free and open market tending to the optimum allocation of scarce resources, while at the same time tending to maximize consumer satisfaction. What must be recognized, however, is the strength of the barriers to this process, not least within the machinery of government in a modern state. We may conclude that the late Professor Kent T Healey, of Yale University, was right when he said, 'It is easier to run a small railroad than a big one', while the growing respect today for the work of Friedrich Hayek has neglected his presentation of the case for small government.

Questions for discussion

1. What is the importance of the entrepreneur?
2. What can we learn from 'the economics of public choice'?
3. What do we mean by 'effective demand'?

6

Externalities and the environment

COSTS AND BENEFITS, PROFIT AND LOSS

Economics, as we said at the start of Chapter 1, is about human behaviour in circumstances of scarcity. If something is not scarce (if it is 'abundant', we might say), then it has no price. Unpolluted fresh air in the countryside has no price in exchange – you cannot buy and sell it. Petrol is scarce and you have to pay for it at the going price in the market. But petrol has a hidden cost which we do not pay at the pump; as the petrol is used, the car's engine emits pollutants which make the surrounding fresh air 'expensive' in terms of people's health. Think now of a road haulier, whose diesel engines have the same effect, and you will see that this cost does not appear on the firm's profit and loss account at the end of the year. That is why we call costs of this kind 'external': they are no less real for being ignored by the business, or by the car driver.

Because external costs (or benefits) do not appear in a company's accounts we say that they are 'not brought to book'. The problem is an ancient one: when a stream was dammed to provide power for a mill wheel it interfered with the carriage of goods by boat, while the boats in turn interfered with the interests of fishermen. In the box is a classic textbook example of the problem of externalities. So long as the railways used steam locomotives there were lineside fires during the summer and autumn, which could spread to the adjoining arable land. It is sometimes possible to have recourse to the civil courts, to seek damages from those responsible for costs of this kind, but it is at best a slow and expensive process, and it may deal only with the local problem, whereas most pollution affects people throughout the community.

EXTERNAL COSTS AND BENEFITS FOR FARMERS

A farmer sows clover after harvest, so as to plough it in when it blooms and enrich the soil. His neighbour keeps bees, and the production of honey is increased as they feed off the clover, but this is a free gift as far as the farmer is concerned; it is an external benefit. In the following year the farmer sprays his field with insecticide, which kills off many of the bees, producing an external cost. Neither way does any money change hands, which is why we speak of externalities.

Environmental pollution is a complex problem. We tend to think of it in terms of road vehicles involved in congestion, but this is a special case. A broad classification might include noise, visual intrusion, local air pollution and the disposal of obsolete vehicles, each of which impose disutilities upon people who suffer from their impact. (Some would add 'light pollution', in that street lighting today makes it difficult to enjoy a starry sky, as well as inhibiting the practice of astronomy.) These costs are imposed upon individuals, but they are very hard to quantify. They may indeed vary from person to person, and a railway enthusiast may actually benefit by living next to a busy main line. They are also a by-product of the demand of transport users for access to services and terminals. Emissions, though, may have a wider impact, by leading to poor health and actual sickness, whose costs are born not only by patients but by the health services which are financed out of general taxation. The same problem applies to the consequences of accidents, to the extent that the insurance concerned fails to cover the wider costs. And finally there is the direct impact of emissions on the environment, where the calculations are even more problematic because of the debate concerning such problems as global warming, upper-level ozone depletion and the incidence of acid rain.

There is often pressure for government intervention to set the balance right. Allowing more road freight deliveries to supermarkets at night could be justified by the reduction of congestion in the daytime. But apart from the problems identified in public choice theory, which we examined in Chapter 5, intervention may lead to further externalities. The clean air legislation of the 1960s led to the closure of furnaces throughout the Black County in the West Midlands, with consequent unemployment and the loss of skills valuable in the economy. Where it can be achieved, the alternative is to take steps to internalize the costs that can be identified.

In the State of California a law was passed requiring that motor vehicles cease to emit pollutants by a given date. The consequence was to raise the price and running cost of cars, buses and trucks by a figure roughly reflecting the original external cost. In the United Kingdom, government has laid down certain minimum emission standards and has introduced various engineering requirements, such as the use of catalytic converters in motor exhaust systems. It has also subsidized the development and introduction of cleaner fuels and new energy systems, although this cannot be seen as internalizing costs; indeed, it is rather the reverse. It must be remembered that there can be no such thing as zero pollution, and eventually the cost of further intervention cannot be justified by the additional benefit.

THE PROBLEM OF TRACK COSTS

There is however one specific set of external costs that lends itself to correction. This is the widespread congestion that we experience on urban roads and streets as well as on interurban highways and motorways. It is a major contributor to environmental pollution, and it leads to a serious waste of both human and physical resources. It is a cost that the road user both experiences and imposes on others, and it is extremely doubtful whether anything short of internalizing it will make it go away. Because it is of fundamental importance for all modes of transport we shall examine it more fully in Part Two, Chapter 8, but some analysis of the problem will be helpful here.

Railway companies pay for the use of rail track. Airlines pay for the use of terminals, and shipping companies pay for the use of ports. Communication by telephone or the Internet is not cost-free. Roads and bridges, though, which are very expensive to build and to maintain, are provided by central or local government, out of what is called 'the general fund of taxable income'. Contrary to most people's belief, the taxes we pay in order to use the roads are not set aside to provide and maintain the road system; HM Treasury collects all the money, along with all forms of taxation, and government then decides how it can be spent: for defence, the health service, education and all the other calls upon central funds, including transport. In practice we pay substantially more in motor taxation than is used for the roads, while the system makes no attempt to allocate the total revenue in terms of the costs imposed by various classes of vehicle.

The consequence of this practice is that the price we pay for using the roads is zero at the margin, in economic terms. What this means is that it makes no difference to our costs however much or little mileage we do. Clearly this gives an apparent cost advantage to road haulage over rail freight, since for the haulier the use of the road is an externality, while, fuel apart, the tax paid is a fixed cost in the short run. For the private car, whose users are far less cost-conscious than are commercial operators, the roads are in effect a free gift, and it is this that accounts for the problem of congestion that occurs at various times and places all over the system.

Congestion tolls have been used in various countries to deal with the problem, but as a form of intervention they are not easily defended in terms of economics. They are expensive to provide and operate, and they can lead to further congestion, while above all they fail to deal with the situation that exists whereby road users in rural areas are severely overcharged by the present system, while all road users in city centres pay far too little. Neither are they free from the problems associated with public choice theory, which we discussed in Chapter 5. However, the technology exists for a system of electronic point pricing, which would mean that road users would pay according to the costs they impose, including congestion costs. It can be assumed that commercial firms would then adjust their use of road transport accordingly, while motorists would have a strong incentive to find an alternative form of transport, an alternative route or destination, or to travel at a different time of the day or year.

It must be emphasized that road pricing is not another form of taxation, but a system whose effect would be to internalize the costs which are not at present 'brought to book'. Far from tending to improve allocatory efficiency, the present system works against that desirable objective, by leading to the wasteful use of a scarce resource – road space at various times and places, in towns and cities and on the interurban highway network.

TRANSPORT AND THE SCARCITY OF LAND

Land, as we saw in Chapter 1, is one of the factors of production, along with labour and capital. Its relative scarcity is reflected in its price, and while there may appear to be plenty of it, price always reflects the strength of demand. Even countries like Russia and the United States, which have vast quantities of land, have problems of scarcity; for example, in cities. The efficient use of land is therefore a major concern for economic policy, and transport is only one of the industries that are in the market for using it.

The interaction of demand and supply means that the scarcity of land is at its greatest in cities and towns and at its lowest in rural areas. In saying this we neglect for the time being the problem of externalities, and concentrate upon the reasons why an acre of land costs vastly more in the City of London than it does in the open countryside. To begin with, living in towns and cities brings a range of satisfactions that people value and are willing to pay for, and these satisfactions are more close to hand than they are if you live elsewhere. All human history has been marked by the growth of cities, and indeed the word 'civilization' is related to the word city. The pressure is then for the city to be highly compact, so that the concentration of land-use forces up prices. From the late 19th century, first trams, then buses, then the private car have enabled the boundary to spread, but there is a limit to the acreage of a city, beyond which it ceases increasingly to be functional. The development of suburban centres and the amalgamation of neighbouring towns to form conurbations complicates this pattern but does not alter the principle.

This scarce commodity, land, is desired by a wide range of users, among whom transport represents only one element. Others include housing, industrial and commercial users, hospitals and medical centres, buildings required for religious uses, entertainment and education, local and central government and administration, and open space: parks, playing fields, cemeteries and allotments. The fact that transport provision is essential for all of these uses does not give the transport industry any privileged position in the market for urban land.

Not all of these uses lend themselves to the pricing of land, which is of course the way in which the market tends to allocative efficiency. Public parks, for example, would never be used if there had to be an entry price. Imagine what it would cost to go into London's Hyde Park if the revenue had to equal the rental income that would be available if the land were used for commercial and residential buildings, yet any shortfall would be in effect an opportunity cost. Public libraries and many museums are 'free at the point of use', and as with parks and open space, this reflects a general agreement that some things should be available for use in this way, for the general benefit of the community. While churches have to obtain the necessary costs of maintenance from their members, or from endowments, council properties are funded from general taxation. This raises further problems in Britain, where we have a system of property taxation – 'the rates' – which is supposed to reflect land values, but does so ineffectively, since it is subject to political manipulation, combined with a 'business tax', which is dictated by HM Treasury. The system as a whole is confused, and cannot be seen to follow any economic logic.

The fact that land for transport is essential for the functioning of the city does not give it the right to any special priority within the general pricing system, but leaves it in competition with all other users of land as a scarce commodity, the degree of scarcity varying with the concentration of demand and other factors. The market for land, though, is highly imperfect, the problem of the opportunity cost of public open space being one example, and one of the most serious weaknesses arises from the fact that roads, as users of land, have no value in the market, since no one owns them. When railways were built the companies had to buy the land for them, but even where land has been bought by local authorities for road building, the investment does not appear on any balance sheet. It is, in effect, another externality, and it is this, of course, that gives rise to the congestion problems which we have discussed, since what is not owned cannot be charged for on any rational basis. We shall return to this in Chapter 8.

There is another aspect of the problem, which has only recently been discussed: the impact of transport investment on the value of land in other uses. It is a complicated issue. The construction of a by-pass road may be expected to reduce the value of a filling station that depended upon the through traffic, while at the same time it will increase the value of farm land alongside it, some of which can be sold for the construction of a new filling station. Within cities the extension of a tube railway will have the effect of increasing the value of land in the area concerned, often to a very substantial degree, and this increase will be a free gift to the landowners. In the city of Montreal the council financed the construction of a transit line by borrowing the money against the expected increase in income from rates (land taxes), around the stations, that would follow from its opening. We shall return to this in Chapter 11, but for the time being it must be kept in mind as another part of the externalities issue.

A final problem is the use of land for transport purposes outside cities, where its value is lower because there is so much less competition for its use. The poet Wordsworth wrote a sonnet deploring the construction of a railway into the Lake District, and today there is often political opposition to the construction of new roads and the expansion of shipping terminals. The environmental issues involved are extremely difficult to measure, and the demonstrators are all too often unwilling to enter into informed discussion. Here the problem lies in identifying and calculating the externalities, both costs and benefits, but there is no doubt that so long as the roads are free at the point of use it will be very difficult to find a solution.

CONCLUSION

Despite the beneficial tendency of the market to bring about economic efficiency and the satisfaction of effective demand, the transport industry, like any other, is subject to a range of weaknesses that interfere in the process. These are largely the result of circumstances of which the normal costing and pricing decisions cannot or do not take account, so the costs and benefits involved are not brought to book. It is desirable that these externalities be 'internalized' so far as possible in the interest of efficiency and effectiveness, and one major step in this direction would be to introduce a charge, or price, for the use of the roads. Other externalities such as pollution, accident costs, and consequences for the environment more generally may prove more difficult to deal with, and thus give rise to pressure for intervention and statutory control, but it must always be remembered, as we saw in Chapter 5, that intervention by public authority brings with it problems that may even make things worse.

Questions for discussion

1. Are there any external costs that cannot be 'brought to book'?
2. Is traffic congestion an external cost?
3. How can transport compete in the market for land?

7

Transport and public policy

THE STATE OF PUBLIC KNOWLEDGE

A very senior railway manager once said, 'The problem with Britain is that everyone is overworked. They all have two jobs: their own, and running the railway.' There are two issues here, the first being that people generally have little knowledge of the transport industries, which must be the fault of those who work in them, and perhaps do too little to promote public understanding. The second is that people take it for granted that transport services can be relied upon, and they not unreasonably assume that problems are there to be overcome. All the same, as we shall see in Part Two, Chapter 11, railways seem to have a special place in the emotions of many British people, which can make it difficult to have a reasoned discussion of the problems that they face.

The quotation with which we started rings true when you read the letters people write to their local newspaper, and again in what journalists themselves have to say about transport. Perhaps it is because the industry performs an essential function in our society that people expect perfection of transport, while at the same time regarding the industry as dull and uninteresting. Perhaps that is why they think they could run it better if they were in charge.

When we dig a little deeper into the assumptions that often lie within the debate on policy we come to an often unspoken assumption that transport is exempt from the laws of economics. After privatization bus companies were accused of pursuing profit at the expense of the passenger, despite the obvious truth that it is only by serving the passenger that profits can be obtained. There is some political pressure to hold bus and train fares down by means of subsidy, which not only ignores the 'public choice' issues we discussed in Chapter 5, but forgets that price and quality of service are closely related, and that quality may actually matter more to the consumer than price. In any case, subsidy must always weaken the ability of the market to tend to the efficient allocation of scarce resources.

It is also interesting to note the differences in public attitude that exist between the different modes of transport. Civil aviation, deep-sea shipping and most of the cross-channel ferries are highly commercialized, and subsidy is only expected where there are problems of access, as with the outlying Scottish islands (although civil aviation is in effect subsidized since there is no tax on aviation spirit). Perhaps even more noticeable is the extent to which road haulage and distribution, both highly competitive and efficient, are (as we shall see in Chapter 9) unaffected by the 'public service' philosophy that distrusts the market, but desires greater intervention in railways and bus services. The political pressures that lie behind the debate we shall return to later in this chapter, but it is worth examining the extent to which these industries carry out effective marketing, which we shall look at in Part Three.

GOVERNMENT AND POLITICS

The assumption that transport is in some way 'different' from other productive industries, or the retail trade, underlies the interventionist policies of governments that invariably tend to limit the effectiveness of the market process, the catallaxy. While economists accept that safety regulation is justified, but worry about its tendency to intervene to restrict technical developments, the British Parliament has intervened in the commercial activities of railways ever since they were introduced. In most European countries the railways were built by or for the state from the beginning, and there was a school of thought that assumed them to be the equivalent of defence in terms of public spending. In Britain the electric tramways and later the motor bus were given protected status; and in due course public ownership, and the public choice mentality, were extended to the railway industry and two-thirds of the buses.

The thought behind this was based on the argument that we examined in Chapter 1, that economic efficiency can be achieved by centralized control. This can now be seen to have failed, as economics indicates that it must, and there has recently been a return to the market for both trains and buses, one consequence of which has been marked improvement in the satisfaction of effective demand. But there remains a politically sensitive area in which intervention, however it may be justified, must be examined in terms of its effects on the market process.

Today there is much wholly creditable pressure for the reduction of the barriers that face people with disabilities of various kinds, whose interests have been neglected for so many years and in so many ways. The box on page 70 illustrates this, and reminds us that good marketing management should have identified the problem before government intervention became necessary. Only recently have we seen new railways built with level access from the platform to the carriage: why was the gap tolerated for so long? Buses used to be designed by manufacturers without even the operators being given a chance to think about the needs of the passenger, who was probably seen as a fit and capable man, anyway. But it has not been the transport industry alone to be at blame, for the need for wheelchair users to have access to all floors in shops and public buildings, and to be able to cross the street, is a matter that has started to receive attention only in recent years.

EASE OF ACCESS

When buses with low steps were first becoming available, a company carried out a survey of passengers to see how satisfied they were. The answer was that they were fine, but as long as there were steps at the doorways of shops and offices they would make little difference. Good marketing on the part of retailers and a duty of care in government and the public services should have made this plain long ago.

If it is the fault of road and rail passenger transport that government intervention has been seen to be necessary, since the industry did not recognize the problem, we can identify a market failure, and trust that the resulting intervention has not become too great a regulatory failure. But beyond this we have seen in recent years the desire of government to extend this kind of intervention to deal with what is now called social exclusion. This takes us into a highly political area, of great concern for economists, who worry about the implications for the efficiency of the market.

There are two areas of policy here, which overlap. In each case the problem is not so much market failure as the failure of marketing, and in each case the costs of intervention are substantial. The more general area is the requirement that local authorities provide reduced fares on public transport for pensioners and the disabled; the second is rural transport and the attempts to support it, which have only made the problem worse.

In many service industries, such as hairdressing and catering, it is common practice to offer reduced prices to pensioners at periods of low demand, or more generally. This reflects good costing (see Chapter 2), since any additional trade is welcome, while overhead and staff costs continue irrespective of cash flow. British Rail recognized this many years ago, and promotional fares for senior citizens were introduced in out-of-peak periods, to fill empty seats, with no element of subsidy of any kind. There is no pressure upon the retail trade to offer subsidies for pensioners, where the constant downward pressure on prices that follows from competition deals with the matter. Subsidy to bus companies however imposes expensive administrative costs, and complicated calculations as to how far the subsidy brings more passengers. Opinion in the industry is tending to wish that government would end the system, and leave the bus companies to follow the example of the railways.

The objective of this kind of subsidy is to make access to shops, entertainment and public services easier for those with limited incomes, who are seen to be in a sense 'excluded' from such satisfactions. As a political concept it extends to education, public libraries and museums, which are not our concern here. Whether or not it can be justified, the economist must be concerned as to the extent to which it is necessary in transport, and as to its consequences in terms of efficient allocation.

The same principle applies in a different way to the very real problem of rural transport services. This growing problem was neglected for far too long, Parliament having assumed since the late 19th century that railways, and later bus operators, should be required to deal with this by cross-subsidy (see Chapter 2). When belatedly it became plain that such a policy was not viable, government intervened with direct subsidy for rural bus services, but administered it in such a way as to seriously disturb the market and to undermine the fragile economy of local operators, already weakened by the spread of car ownership and use. The issues here were those of market failure in part only, for the heart of the problem lies deeper, but the outcome has been a classic example of regulatory failure.

The non-urban and non-suburban areas of the country have never benefited from the levels of public transport that exist in towns and cities, and such levels indeed could never have been provided outside towns and cities, either commercially or by way of subsidy. After the 1950s the spread of car ownership and the industrialization of agriculture progressively reduced demand for traditional bus services, and the larger companies progressively withdrew from 'deep rural' areas. Today it is true to say that the private car is the most effective form of passenger transport in these areas, yet the burden of taxation is the same wherever people live. Table 7.1 indicates the extent to which rural car users are overcharged whereas car users in cities pay too little for the use they make of the roads.

Table 7.1   Charging for the use of urban and rural roads

Social costs in relation to excess taxation paid, by road type

Road user type	Marginal social costs Index (average 100)	Under- or over-payment in relation to social costs, per km
Motorway	14.6	4.81
Rural	16.1	4.73
Urban, non-central, off-peak	214.8	−6.00
Urban, non-central, peak	366.7	−14.2
Urban, central, off-peak	616.7	−27.7
Urban, central, peak	803.7	−37.8

Note: In 1999 road users paid some £32 billion in total road taxation, while total road expenditure was just under £6 billion. If we assume that the surplus represented external (social) costs we can see from the table how unfairly this burden is distributed among road users, with those using urban roads benefiting at the expense of those who use motorways and rural roads. Only road pricing could correct this imbalance.

Source: Peter Mumford (2000) *The Road from Inequity: Fairer ways of paying the true costs of road use*, Adam Smith Institute.

To the economist, then, the use of public money to subsidize certain sectors of the population, with the objective of reducing what is loosely described as social exclusion, tends to inefficiency in the market. Yet the problem is capable of solution by commercial processes, together with the introduction of road-use pricing. These are but two of the regulatory failures for transport that weaken the beneficial working of the catallaxy.

THE NEGLECTED FACTOR

Economic analysis seeks to identify a market for a given commodity, and we sometimes refer to firms in competition as 'players in the market'. The great mistake of managers in the bus industry and the railways after 1950 was to assume that they were in the market for bus or train passengers as the case might be, when they should have realized that their market is for the carriage of people. Within the British Isles this means that the players in the market include buses and coaches, trains and aircraft, and the private car.

The 'commodity', as we saw in Chapter 1, is safe arrival at the individual's desired destination, and the circumstances of price and quality are secondary, though very important to understand. As we saw, the demand for transport is always derived from the demand for other satisfactions, obtainable 'somewhere else'. We might almost say that the demand is for 'instantaneous transposition', and that the ideal would be to be able to get into a vehicle here, and get out there, now.

This book is about transport and economic policy, not public transport and economic policy. Yet much debate about transport policy neglects the obvious fact that the private car is just another form of transport. We shall see in Part Two, Chapter 8 the importance of understanding the price of the infrastructure, and Chapter 10 is about the market for movement, but first we must ask why it is that the private car is widely seen to be something different.

The answer lies in policy: industrial and employment policy. The bus and train companies have to buy their rolling stock in the market, and the capital cost is related to the economy in general, with little intervention on the part of government, subsidies excepted. Cars are assembled in factories all over the world, and the market for cars is highly competitive, while the industry employs large numbers of people. There is a great deal of both capital and labour tied up in car assembly, and in the manufacturing processes that provide the components for the plants to assemble, with the raw materials that are required at each stage. Car construction, then, is a very large industry, and plays a large part in the economy of every country in which such plants are to be found.

The transport industry is built round economies of scale, which we examined in Chapter 1. It therefore depends upon the ability of manufacturers to obtain the necessary cash flow that can justify the very large investment in such plants, and this means keeping prices down and selling as many cars as possible. This in turn means that the product must have a relatively short working life, so that new cars are constantly being ordered, while the older ones are sold on the secondhand market ('cascaded') until safety regulations ensure that they are scrapped.

One consequence of this is that the market for movement, by all modes, is distorted by the sales pressure of the private car sector. The pressure is always on to sell more cars, and this ensures that there are always plenty of them on the market, and some of them are very cheap. If the owner-driver is a mechanic, then operating cost is very low as well, and there is a highly competitive market for spare parts. The true cost of motoring (after allowing for changes in the value of money) has remained steady for some years. For these reasons, before considering the utility of the private car, we are faced with a remarkable distortion in the overall passenger transport market, and it is a phenomenon that is too easily ignored. Sometimes the biggest problems are the easiest to forget about.

CONCLUSION

The often unspoken assumption that transport, and especially passenger transport, is unlike other industries and so is not suited to economic analysis, combined with the emotional attitude people often show when railways are in the news, cannot be allowed to be left without criticism. But this is a highly political subject, and, perhaps because of these attitudes, it is often assumed that 'government' must be made responsible for getting everything working perfectly. It is interesting to see how much media attention there is to a railway accident, while no notice is taken of the loss of life, and the public and private financial costs associated with road transport, and particularly to the private car. As we turn to apply the economic principles that have been discussed in Part One to the operations of the transport modes, we shall have to remember always this ignorance of the facts of the matter, which assumes that economics has nothing to say about transport policy. By now it must be plain that this is simply not true.

Questions for discussion

1. What are the duties of government regarding transport?
2. Would it be better for subsidy to go to operators or to users?
3. What is the market for the product of the transport industries?

Part two

Applying the template

8

General problems of the infrastructure

THE TEMPLATE

In Part One we examined the economics of transport, and in Chapters 2 to 6 we went into greater depth with regard to the essential issues – costing, pricing, efficiency, effectiveness and externalities. Taken together, we can see these as a 'template' against which the performance of the various modes of inland transport may be analysed, and so in Part Two we shall undertake this in four operational areas. First, however, we have to take account of one fundamental problem which will crop up throughout our discussions: the distortions in the market that follow from the pricing of the infrastructure (the roads or rails upon which vehicles run). Since the key economic objectives of allocative efficiency and consumer effectiveness cannot fully be achieved, as we shall see, the multitudinous decisions made in the market cannot be fully rational.

TRACK, TERMINALS AND SIGNALLING

Long established in railway parlance, these three words sum up the meaning of transport infrastructure, and can be used to analyse the relative advantages and disadvantages of the various modes. Thus track costs for sea transport are nonexistent, which gives coastwise shipping an advantage over road or rail for bulk movements, but seaports are expensive terminals. The air is also free for use, but air terminals again are expensive, and so is air traffic control. For all modes of transport terminals have to be paid for, either directly, or by way of capital cost (opportunity cost) and expenses if they are owned by the user. Railways incur direct costs for their signalling, but traffic signals on the roads are part of public expenditure, as is the supervision of safety, or 'quality control', which we examined in Chapter 4.

On the whole the market works efficiently for terminals and signalling, although the money raised by the airport tax that passengers pay is not directly linked to the cost of air traffic control. Indeed, like all taxes, it goes into the Treasury's general fund of taxable income, and when all the government's income is put together, the 'spending departments' – primarily defence, education, health and transport – are allocated their shares in the Budget by the Chancellor of the Exchequer (which are never as much as each had asked for). Some of the money for transport is used for bus and rail subsidy, but the most important part provides for the roads, and for them, as will be plain, there is no direct charge at all. Expenditure is the responsibility of the highway authorities and the contractors employed for the motorway system, and road users have little or no control over how it is applied, and little or no redress if the roads are neglected.

In some parts of the country there are privately owned toll roads or bridges, where the user has to pay for each trip, and direct charges are made for some bridges and tunnels for which the government is responsible, although these are intended just to repay the investment involved in their construction. Something similar applies to the idea of privately constructed motorways, where the company will be able to collect tolls over a period of years, after which ownership will revert to the state. But any suggestion of making road users pay for the 'track' over which they move, as the train operating companies have to, is met with public outrage.

TRACK COSTS AND PRICING

For most of our purchases there comes a time when we decide it is not worth spending any more for one more unit of supply. In economics this is what is called the 'marginal price', because a decrease in the unit price (or, rather, in the mix of price and quality) might make it worth spending after all. Sometimes, as when we buy a travel pass which gives an unlimited number of trips within a given period, there is no marginal price per trip, and we do not think twice whether to consume another unit of supply. This is because the company finds it worthwhile to obtain our payment 'upfront', and the price is based on marketing evidence of the average number of trips that are likely to be made. If we make more, then we have benefited by a discount, much as we do when a retailer offers 'two for the price of one'. Of course, the 'true cost' catches up with us when we have to buy another pass, or renew our phone card, but broadly speaking the bargain we have entered into is a commercial one, which means that on the whole both supplier and consumer are content with the deal.

It may help if we compare the way we pay for the supply of electricity with the charge made for water, in the absence of a domestic water meter. Electricity is priced per unit, so we pay for as much or as little as we use, and if we are 'economical' we see that unnecessary lights are turned off. Water, on the other hand, is free at the point of use, and we feel little need to economize. A dripping tap is not a cost in the way a light bulb is when it is left on. Another example is the telephone, where we tend to forget about the marginal price until the bill comes in at the end of the quarter.

All of this brings us to the problem of the marginal price for the use of track for inland transport. If you go by train a certain element of your fare goes direct from the train operating company to pay for the use of the rails, and the same applies to the cost of a consignment of freight. If you use the public roads, no part of what you pay goes direct to the cost of providing them. You do not actually pay anything, per mile, for the journey you make or for the carriage of your goods. So you have no incentive to 'economize', as you have for the electric light or the telephone. Instead we have what in economics is known as zero marginal price. An extra mile costs nothing, so you do not ask yourself 'is it worth it?' No wonder the roads and highways are congested! Indeed, as we saw in Chapter 6, congestion gives rise to external costs, which again are not charged to the users of the roads.

The contrast between rail and road track prices lies in the fundamental distinction that no one owns the roads. That is to say, there is no figure representing their capital cost on any balance sheet. Even where public money has been spent to buy land for road building, it is not expected to earn any interest to cover the investment; in other words, we have no measure of the opportunity cost of the roads. This is clearly a serious distortion of the national economy, and along with the problem of zero marginal price it means that the costs of the transport industry are similarly distorted. The box explains how it works.

THE ROADS ARE YOURS!

The legal definition of a highway is a path over which all members of the public have liberty to pass and repass for business or pleasure. It has nothing to do with who owns the land over which the public may pass, and no payment is due. It is a 'right of passage', and we should remember that freedom to come and go as we please is a very basic right, and one that has been abused in the past in some countries. *Laissez-passer* is as important as *laissez-faire* in defining the liberty of the subject. Strictly speaking, the owner of property adjoining the highway also owns the land up to the mid-point of the road, but there is no way in which the user of the highway can be charged for travelling on it. At least, that is how the law stands now.

The provision of dedicated space for parking of vehicles is an area of policy where little economic rationality can be discerned. A distinction must be made between the provision of purpose-built space and parking on the highway. For most off-street parking, the opportunity cost of both the land and the construction, together with charges for maintenance and operation, should be provided for by the hourly rate, which may be expected to vary according to demand, and to reflect the degree of security offered to the customer. Parking charges at air and rail terminals and entertainment centres may be expected to reflect similar requirements, combined with the need to provide for access to the services concerned, on open land as well as in covered accommodation. (We shall return to the subject of 'park and ride' in Chapter 10.) Where land in urban areas is derelict, awaiting development, a temporary income can be obtained by charging 'what the traffic will bear'.

Parking on the highway, or on land in the ownership of local authorities, presents a different situation. The public highway, as we have seen, is not a property in any meaningful sense, but rather carries a 'right of passage', so it must be doubtful whether any strict right exists for its use as a 'warehouse', by those who stand vehicles on it. The fact that no capital value is attached to it, so that its opportunity cost is impossible to calculate, and that there is no form of pricing for its use, raises complications to which we shall return. Nevertheless it *is* used for 'parking', giving rise to conflicts of interest between residential users, those who desire access to other sites, and the normal movement of traffic.

There is no easy way out of this problem, which has arisen with the spread of car ownership throughout the community. But local authorities have responsibilities for the highway, and they have sought to discharge these by prohibiting parking on certain kerb-sides, and permitting it in others, usually with a time limit; a compromise solution with consequent problems of enforcement. Faced with this the economist, recognizing a scarcity situation, varying by time and place, would look to some form of pricing to tend to the optimum use of this scarce resource.

This has led to the introduction of parking meters, still with problems of enforcement, but which appear to be the rational way of dealing with the problem. Policy hinges, though, on the objective of the pricing regime, which opens itself to criticism when the charges continue in periods of little or low demand for space. Since the highway is still, in whatever sense, 'public property', what may be called rationing by price would seem to be rational and justified where and when scarcity exists, but to continue to charge beyond such a state of affairs appears to be mere profit-seeking at the expense of the user, whether the user is a motorist, haulier or coaching firm.

What is less often noticed is the practice of both private business and public authorities in seeking to enforce a condition of contract or a by-law that prohibits the transfer of parking tickets. Since the user has in effect purchased a defined space for a specified period of time, it would seem that a commodity has been obtained in return for payment, which should be transferable as a free gift, and indeed – though this is rare – at a price. Bus and train operators have for many years sought to apply a similar condition on the sale of tickets, but marketing policy has led to the issue of family tickets and other shared purchases. Where payment is made on exit from the car park, or 'on foot' from a machine, the situation would not seem to arise, but wherever charges are based on 'pay and display' the restriction of transfer must appear to be contrary to the benefit of the public in the use of public open space on (or near) the highway.

When (and if) point-of-use road pricing (see below) is introduced, the whole logic of parking prices will have to be confronted, but for the time being we should recognize that the economist's concern with scarcity can, and indeed should, be brought to bear upon the problems that exist already.

EFFICIENCY, EFFECTIVENESS AND EXTERNALITIES

Because the market for land is ineffective where highways are concerned, there is no way in which the provision and maintenance of roads and motorways can be seen to tend to the efficient allocation of scarce resources. A similar problem arose when railways were built, and landowners could hold out for exorbitant prices, even though Parliament sought to intervene. It has been known for public money to be put into the purchase of land for road improvements, and yet the new construction has been delayed for as much as 50 years, with the land yielding no return on the investment. New road building from the 1960s on was based on a 'predict and provide' policy, with social cost/benefit studies that were open to adjustment to satisfy political requirements. Highway and land-use planning have never been systematically related, and while some new roads have become overcrowded within months of their opening, others have remained under-used.

The problems of congestion make plain the extent to which highway management fails to achieve the economic objective of satisfying effective demand. We shall turn to the consequences of that failure in Chapters 9 and 10. Attempts to internalize external costs have failed, largely for reasons of a highly charged political nature. However hard it may be to calculate the requirements of economic efficiency, externalities of two kinds tend to introduce irrational factors into the debate. To begin with we have the NIMBY argument – not in my back yard – which comes from the middle classes and has blocked the construction of new railways as well as new roads, while alongside this there are the environmentalists who are frequently unwilling to see that there are benefits as well as costs involved in the construction of new motorways and bypasses.

To the economist the problem lies in the lack of any system of exchange, because of the absence of measurable values in the use of land for transport. Even so, externalities will always be a problem, and it is to be hoped that those who remind us of them will engage in less highly charged political activity in the future. Within towns and cities there can never be enough land for it to be used for free, but the roads are treated as if that were the case. In tourist areas, as we shall see in Chapter 12, there are very similar problems, but in the countryside in general there cannot be unlimited land available for road – or railway – construction to go on without measurement of the costs and benefits. Such measurement is very difficult to achieve unless it is brought home to the consumer.

ROAD-USE PRICING

The problem is further complicated by the economics of the motor industry, which we examined in Chapter 7, and shall return to in Chapter 10. There is however a possible solution for it, which was first proposed by a government report – the Smeed Report – in 1964. All that has changed since then is that the technology has become more effective, but the principles remain the same, and members of the economics profession support the idea with few exceptions.

Public debate on road-use pricing has been complicated by the tendency to speak of it as 'congestion charging', and the assumption that it would involve the use of tolls, such as those proposed for central London. The idea is also resisted because of the general assumption that 'we pay enough for our roads already', whereas, as we have seen, we just pay taxes – and the total of road taxation comes to considerably more than the amount actually spent on the roads. The answer to these objections could well be the reduction of some part of this taxation, to offset the point-of-use charging system recommended by the Smeed Report. The relief of congestion that would undoubtedly follow from charging is highly desirable, but the object of the exercise is to enable road users to make rational decisions, and so to improve the efficiency of the market for movement.

The present system is also very unfair, as can be seen from Table 7.1, since transport users in urban areas pay more than is reasonable for the use of roads, while those who live in rural areas, who are far more dependent upon the private car, are heavily overcharged. It has been suggested that vehicle excise duty (VED) should be remitted with respect to cars registered in rural areas, but there are obvious problems associated with this, and it might be better if VED were withdrawn altogether, as a quid pro quo for the introduction of road-use pricing. What matters most, though, is to stress that we are not talking about a tax, but about the price of a scarce commodity – road space at certain times and places. As we saw in Chapter 1, when things are scarce, their price is expected to increase, yet here we have something that is scarce and also without price. Only if we are aware of the price for the commodity on offer, and can set it against the quality, can we take rational decisions as to whether or not we want it enough to pay for it.

This is where tolls have a limited effect, although they have a part to play where the cost of new investment is recovered from users who gain a benefit from it. The use of tolls to raise money with which to subsidize public transport weakens the efficiency of the market by introducing a form of cross-subsidy, while it is bound to appear as a tax, and not as a price. The policy we have inherited from the Smeed Report is the use of electronic point-pricing, bringing home to the user something nearer to the true cost of using congested sections of road, whether urban, interurban or intercity.

PAY AS YOU GO

To tend to improved economic efficiency and the greater effectiveness of the highways in satisfying demand, it would be possible to require road users to install a quite cheap form of meter in their vehicles, containing a form of smart card, precharged with a sum of money. When the vehicle passed a pricing point, probably identified by satellite, a sum of money would be deducted from the smart card, while a sound would inform the driver that a charge had been made. The meter would be designed to show a visible signal if the smart card were fully 'decremented', which would be a criminal offence. In this way the true price of using congested highway space would be brought home, and alternatives would come to be considered: changing the time of the trip, or the route; using public transport; or perhaps walking or cycling.

Congested roads are not only to be found in city centres, and the use of alternatives such as 'rat runs' through residential streets could effectively be discouraged, as could the movement of traffic off motorways and on to the rural road system. Introduction of such a system could be eased by encouraging users to fit the meter (a reduction in VED could be provided for) and then running it without charge, but with the signal sounding, for a year or so to show what the costs would be when charging was introduced.

To tend to the desired improvement in the allocation of scarce resources, which goes to the heart of the problem, pricing would need to be universal. Perhaps only the fire and ambulance services should be exempt. Operators of scheduled bus and coach services would be able to commute the charge by a monthly payment, but as the levels of congestion decreased this would be progressively reduced. While a small increase in the cost of living has been predicted, this would just internalize the external costs which the present system imposes upon us all. It is sometimes objected that such a system would be unfair on the less well off, since they would not be able to afford usage for which the better off would be able to pay, but the better off would no doubt be careful with their money, and the benefits we shall examine in Chapter 10 would apply in different ways to people of all classes.

CONCLUSION

The further implications of the current inefficiencies relating to the infrastructure for freight and passenger transport will be examined in the next few chapters, but no study of the economics of transport can disregard this problem, which distorts the whole catallactic process. Linked to the economics of the motor car industry, which we studied in Chapter 7, the outcome is a problem that appears so large and politically so dangerous that it is all too often ignored. At the heart of it lies a major contradiction: there is a direct price for using rail track, but nothing like it for the roads. This is an ancient problem, for the opposition to Turnpike Trusts, which in the past led on occasion to rioting, illustrates the depth of feeling underlying the assumption that roads ought to be free at the point of use. Looking to the future, there is a strong economic argument for the roads to be 'owned' by non-profit-making companies, so that their true value appears on a balance sheet, and the distortions in the economy that at present exist can finally be removed.

Questions for discussion

1. How do transport firms pay for 'track, terminals and signalling'?
2. What is wrong with the present system?
3. How can we expect motorists to pay for the use of the roads?

9

Freight transport and distribution

BUSINESS LOGISTICS

The use of the term 'logistics' has been avoided so far, because a certain confusion exists as to its definition and its relationship with transport. Transport is essential to the success of supply-chain management, and in that context logistics depends upon transport, rather than transport upon logistics. Nevertheless there is a logistical process that originates with the factors of production and leads to the delivery of transport services, freight or passenger. We shall come up against a similar problem when we consider tourism and hospitality management in Chapter 12. 'Business logistics' is a broader term, extending to the efficiency of the firm as it seeks to achieve objectives, and can include insurance, resource management (including human resources and the supply-chain), purchasing and supply, packaging, marketing, and of course transport. It is thus the key to success in any business, and the point at which all the departments of the firm interact. The product of the firm, whether it is goods or services, must satisfy the effective demand of the consumer as to price and quality, which is where the entre-preneur comes in, and in the case of goods the end of the chain must be delivery (which of course may be the consumer carrying the goods home in a car).

Logistics in this sense, then, is part of the catallaxy, and its importance lies in the extent to which it tends to both the achieve-ment of allocative efficiency and the satisfaction of effective demand. In this it is served by the availability of transport, both for the movement of people, so that employees and customers can have access to the firm and its products, and for the movement of goods through the supply chain, within the production process, and in the eventual delivery of goods to the customer. In this chapter we examine the market for movement in terms of the movement of goods, by applying each of the terms of our template and investi-gating how far the industry satisfies the expectations we have identified for it under each of these headings: costing, pricing, allocative efficiency, consumer effectiveness, and externalities.

BACKGROUND AND ORGANIZATION

In today's economy this market is dominated by road transport. Contrary to the general public belief, road haulage was not destroyed by the canals or the railways; it has played a significant part in trade since the 17th century, when the nation's political economy began to stabilize, and it has continued to do so as part of the wider transport industry that included coastwise shipping, inland water-ways and later also canals, and then the railways. As each mode of transport developed it benefited from its comparative advantage, and the railway age which replaced the canal age gave way in its turn to the motor transport age, commencing in the 1950s.

The essential advantage of road haulage over the canals and railways was that it could provide door to door collection and delivery services, while much goods movement within industrial cities was in horse-drawn vehicles until the motor vehicle came along. The pattern changed radically in the second half of the 20th century, as the nation's economy shifted from heavy industry to lighter manufacturing. Steel and coal play a very much smaller part in the industry of the developed world today, and bulk haulage therefore plays a smaller part as well. Railways have concentrated more and more on providing fast inter-city services, and the standards of the permanent way needed for such traffic do not permit the retention of sidings to serve industrial plant along the tracks; neither could every small manufacturing plant justify a branch line. Even rail-served trading estates like that built at Slough in the 1930s do not enable the railways to offer services as efficient as those of the road freight distribution industry. By the 1970s the term 'physical distribution management' was being used to define this rapidly expanding sector of the transport industry.

The business of distribution that is so important today was made possible by the construction of the motorways and the improvement of the trunk road system. It is often forgotten that the government decided to develop motorways for industry, and not for the private car. As the modern road system developed after the 1950s it enabled trucks and vans to carry goods from point to point, with no break of bulk, and with reliable schedules. This was a service that the railway could not offer. After a period during which railways seemed to be withdrawing from the freight market, privately owned rail freight companies have started to build up traffic in medium to long distance bulk traffic, and the abolition of the National Dock Labour Scheme has enabled some movement to coastwise shipping. But Table 9.1 shows what a high proportion of freight moves by road in this country today.

Ownership of the industry today, the Post Office apart, lies in the private sector, and the road transport firms are predominantly small in scale, although many one-person businesses work on contract to larger operators. Vehicles in such firms may work away from base, especially in the tipper trade, where you find work where you can get it. As we shall see in Part Three, a highly competitive industry such as this one requires marketing decisions to be taken by managers close to the customers, and this offsets any economies of scale that might encourage concentration of ownership. Much of the maintenance and support side is 'outsourced' by the movement operators, while many trucks that carry the insignia of supermarket businesses are owned and operated by contractors. The industry is very much involved in international movement,

Table 9.1 Freight transport by mode, 1998–99

Mode	Goods moved (billion tonne/km and %)		Goods lifted (million tonnes and %)	
		%		%
Road (all goods vehicles)	156.7	65	1661	81
Rail	18.4	8	103	5
Water*	53.0	22	143	7
Pipeline	11.6	5	155	8

Note: * Figures for all UK traffic, including Northern Ireland, thus over-stating the Great Britain coastwise trade. The small proportion of rail carriage in the total is plain.

Source: Transport Statistics Great Britain 2000, The Stationery Office

throughout Europe and beyond, and haulage firms based in other member states of the European Union can and do carry loads entirely within the United Kingdom. The British motorway system also forms a 'land bridge' for the movement of goods between Ireland and the European mainland.

COSTING AND PRICING

In such a highly competitive industry, with a large proportion of small firms, many of whom at any one time may be at the margin of profitability, a knowledge of costs is essential for survival. While the small businessperson is probably unaware of the term 'opportunity cost', the need to allow for it is constantly present. The size of the fleet may vary, trucks being sold in periods of low demand, and replaced when there is more need for them. Owners of small firms may well carry their knowledge of costs in their head, or in a pocket-book, and it is this that will form the basis for pricing for a new contract. For the small firm the business is its own cost centre, so that the degree of sophistication required by larger businesses can be escaped. Cost-centre costing comes into its own in larger firms, and in rail and sea transport. Terminal costs may be relatively high, especially in the distribution industry, where the 'hub and spoke' organization requires more or less specialized buildings. Rail freight companies pay directly for the use of the track and signalling, and shipping firms pay dues to port companies, but road transport firms, as we have seen in Chapter 8, are subject to no direct charge for the use of their track.

Competition by its nature drives down prices, which must then tend to greater efficiency. But there can be no mathematical formula that will convert cost data to a rigid pricing schedule; decisions have always to be taken in the light of what competitors' prices might be for similar contracts. It is not unknown for the basis for making a quotation to be the cost per day for a vehicle, rather than the cost per mile. New custom may be attracted by keeping the margin low, in the hope that once a contract is secured, the price can be raised in small steps, so long as the customer does not want to go to the trouble of obtaining an alternative supplier. In the parcels and distribution business it is usual to offer a range of prices, depending upon the guaranteed time of delivery, ranging from immediate despatch by courier service, through timed delivery (eg by 10 am next day, or on a specified day of the week) to a maximum of two days or so.

As we have seen in Chapter 3, price and quality are closely related, and the element of quality has become increasingly important for freight movement since the development of 'just in time' (JIT) control in much of industry. This is linked to inventory cost, which we discussed in Chapter 2, which requires the delivery of consignments at pre-agreed times, to ensure the maintenance of minimal but essential stocks. In many such cases the customer will be a stock holder, who deals with the ultimate user, and who must be able to provide supplies on demand. The logistical processes of a supermarket chain require similar control of deliveries, but in principle this is the same as providing guaranteed deliveries to a steel stock holder. The effect of highway congestion, not least on the motorways, plays a serious part in the costing and thus the pricing of trade of this kind, where one case of missed delivery may put the operator's contract at risk.

For some one-off contracts there is what is known as the back-load problem. This is a problem in escapable cost. Thus a firm in a provincial city may have a contract with a customer to deliver goods to an address in London. If the price is based on the round trip, then the escapable cost for the return journey must be zero, and any load that can be obtained, up to the average cost per mile for the trip, will make a positive contribution to the overhead costs of the firm. This can lead to the undercutting of prices, which will damage the profitability of firms based at, in this case, the London end. (The problem may of course arise the other way about.) What is more, back-load agencies exist, to which drivers can go to seek such a contract, and opportunities appear on Web sites. The practice can lead to much ill-feeling in the trade. For many years the practice was banned for cross-boundary traffic within the European Union (EU) and its predecessors, but now the market is open, and a UK van or truck can carry a back-load even within another country's territory. This is called cabotage, and vehicles from other EU states may take advantage of it here, despite the fact that the lower taxes in their home countries give them a significant advantage. (The 2002 UK Budget included proposals to control this unfair situation.)

ALLOCATIVE EFFICIENCY

Road freight transport in the United Kingdom finds itself in a fairly contestable market (see Chapter 1). A sole trader, partnership or firm that can find the necessary capital can set up in business, buying or renting its rolling stock, provided the vehicles satisfy the safety regulations. Everything then depends upon the unladen weight of the vehicles, since European Commission regulations require firms running lorries above 3.5 tonnes unladen weight to hold a valid Operators' Licence (O Licence – see the box on page 95). This introduces an element of planning control, which may be necessary in the UK situation, but can act as a barrier, though there are few commercial activities today to which it does not apply. What is equally important in the definition of contestability is the ability to leave the market, and this is not constrained. Operation itself – productivity – is subject to further regulation, particularly in terms of drivers' working hours and the weight and distribution of the load, and in each of these areas the licensing authority can penalize firms that break the rules. Where a vehicle is stopped and it is found that the load is too great or not distributed over the axles as the regulations require, the driver is liable as well as the operator, and the same thing applies if the tachograph shows that drivers' hours regulations have been broken.

THE OPERATOR'S LICENCE

Firms operating road freight vehicles that exceed 3.5 tonnes unladen weight must obtain an Operator's Licence (O Licence), with very few specialized exemptions. There are three categories:

1. The Standard National Licence (applies where freight is carried for customers entirely within the UK).
2. The Standard International Licence (applies where freight is carried for customers internationally, including within the UK).
3. The Restricted Licence (applies where the only goods carried are in connection with the firm's own business, whether national or international).

An applicant must fulfil certain key criteria, and these standards must be maintained during the life of the licence. They are:

1. To be of 'good repute' (thus certain criminal convictions or an individual's bankruptcy would bar an applicant).
2. To be 'of appropriate financial standing' (this means sufficient cash or credit to be able to maintain the vehicles properly, and to continue to trade).
3. To hold, or to employ a manager who holds, a Certificate of Professional Competence appropriate to the type of licence (this requires passing an examination or holding some equivalent qualification).

The regional licensing authority that issues and enforces the licence must be satisfied as to the adequate provision for maintaining drivers' hours and other standards, and must assess the suitability of the operating centre where the vehicles are kept. All of these provisions apply equally to the bus and coach industry, but for freight transport it is possible for objections to a licence application to be lodged by police and local authorities, trade unions and trade associations, and people or businesses that might be affected by the siting of the depot on environmental grounds. In addition, drivers of large goods vehicles (LGVs) and passenger carrying vehicles (PCVs) must hold an appropriate driving licence and comply with regulations for drivers' hours and records. Vehicles, both freight and passenger, are subject to the Construction and Use Regulations, to an annual test and to inspections at the roadside or at the operator's premises.

These regulatory practices impose a severe constraint on the economic freedom of firms operating heavy goods vehicles (HGVs), while those operating lighter vehicles are subject to little more than the regulations that apply to private cars. The need for quality control is generally accepted, but to the economist the system must still be recognized to be an imperfection in the market. Everything then depends upon the equity with which the regulations are designed and administered, and the potential of regulatory failure is always present, along with the problems of public choice theory, which we examined in Chapter 7. The cost in management terms of satisfying the increasing detail of the regulations forms a very real limitation for the entrepreneur. But what is remarkable is the absence of any such regulation for smaller goods vehicles (this is of course the home of the 'white van').

The degree of contestability is the first criterion for judging the allocative efficiency of any industry, and while the O Licence system places a limit upon entry to the trade, exit is open, and we may conclude that the industry tends to efficiency thus far. No form of price control has ever been made to work for road freight transport, because of its highly competitive nature. The constant downward pressure on prices (sometimes called rates) tends also to efficiency, and affects competitive modes, such as rail freight and coastwise shipping. If that were all there was to it we could be satisfied as to the efficiency of the industry, but there remains one serious limitation, the pricing of the infrastructure, which we discussed in Chapter 6.

For the provision and maintenance of an essential part of the equipment to be taken away from the firm and provided by the state forms a fundamental barrier to the pricing of output so as to reflect total operating cost. Apart from fuel consumption and wages it makes no difference whether a haulier uses a motorway at times of congestion, or moves at night, as the trunk parcels delivery firms do; the cost is the same, and it ranks as an overhead cost because it is paid through taxation. There is no relationship between the income from this taxation and the amount that is spent by government on roads; indeed the state takes far more in tax than it spends. The result is to distort the price/quality relationship so that the tendency to efficiency is negative at this point, because the cost of this essential input is zero at the margin, and so cannot influence decisions in the market.

CONSUMER EFFECTIVENESS

As we would expect, the competitive nature of the industry provides continuing pressure to ensure that the interests of the consumer receive priority. Because it is so important for decisions to be taken by managers or proprietors who are close to the market, firms tend to remain small, and the larger ones have to design their management structure so as to follow the rule. Over its history the road freight industry has seen firms grow too large, and either disappear or be restructured. Subcontracting and franchising are common, especially in distribution, and the logistical requirements of many firms in the manufacturing sector and in retail trade are frequently outsourced in this way. Franchise forms a significant part of the collection and delivery element in parcels and distribution, and firms whose vehicles are too small to require an O Licence are well placed for this kind of work.

Because the regulation of the industry provides for little politically biased intervention there is little or no conflict between the pursuit of efficiency and the pursuit of effectiveness, and the problems that we identified in Chapter 5 regarding public choice theory arise only in the context of road construction, design and maintenance. As in the case of efficiency, infrastructure problems place limits on the ability of firms in road haulage and distribution to pursue customer satisfaction. Severe and often unpredictable congestion makes scheduling difficult. Local highway authorities can have an element of prejudice toward trucks, and there is considerable ignorance in the public mind as to the importance of the industry, whose strength has always been summed up by the marketing slogan 'Serving All Sites', a facility that the railway cannot emulate. It is in the potential development of e-commerce that problems must be anticipated, since local authorities are currently planning to limit vehicle access to some suburban roads. It is too easily forgotten that the highway is itself an essential aspect of the catallaxy, and the absence of commercial costing and pricing for this element weakens the whole economy of movement.

EXTERNALITIES AND THE ENVIRONMENT

The most obvious cost that is difficult to 'bring to book' for the road freight transport firm is air pollution arising from the use of hydrocarbon fuels. Controversy continues about the environmental damage that arises from diesel engines, but whatever the risk, may be it is only through intervention that the costs can be internalized. This means taxation, but it also means enforcement of standards of engine maintenance, which is the responsibility of the licensing system (and is thus a cost in itself.) The effect is to increase the price of transport, and so of goods to the consumer, but while this may impose a limit on consumer effectiveness, it is not in itself a constraint on the allocatory efficiency of the industry. Much depends on getting the balance right, and it would be better if the more emotional attitudes we hear about were treated with reserve. Government intervention is encouraging the development of new forms of motive power, and in due course we may hope that the scale of the problem will be greatly reduced.

Most of the remaining externalities are related to the shortage of land, which we discussed in Chapter 6. Most obvious is the problem of noise, which also arises from railway movement, and while the heavy goods vehicle of today is no doubt quieter than once was the case, the combined volume of traffic noise brings problems, on both urban streets and motorways. Measures to limit movement by night in urban areas must have some effect on efficiency and effectiveness, which may be a small price to pay for the cross-benefit to residents, but for motorway traffic there seems little alternative to building walls or berms to act as baffles where there is residential property close to the road. This of course brings us up against the problem of infrastructure costs and prices, which we have seen to be central to the economics of the industry.

In the same way, congestion is a byproduct of the system whereby roads are free at the point of use. It is peculiar in that the costs are carried both by the vehicles that cause it and those that suffer by it, and at present it is in no one's interest to be the first to remove a vehicle from the congested street. Clearly, the most efficient way to deal with problems of this kind is to introduce point-of-use road pricing, such as we examined in Chapter 6.

PUBLIC ATTITUDES AND PUBLIC POLICY

The word 'juggernaut' has no more specific meaning for an HGV than the word 'jumbo' has for an aeroplane, yet it is frequently used with an emotional charge to refer to trucks that are in some way seen to be undesirable. There are protests whenever maximum dimensions are increased, with the consequence that what might be a straightforward policy decision, based on some degree of calculation, becomes a political 'issue'. Car drivers have no love for the HGV, whose speed is limited both by law and by the installation of vehicle speed limiters. As we have seen, the fact that the motorway system was justified in the first place by the need for the more efficient movement of goods, and that its use for industry may well contribute more to allocatory efficiency than its use for personal movement, is not widely appreciated today. The negative image of the white van (or the 'white van man') is another example of the widespread ignorance of the general public concerning the one branch of transport that perhaps contributes most to its material satisfaction.

Much of public policy is governed by regulation from the European Commission, which is an area where public choice theory gives rise to considerable criticism. Current problems follow from differences between UK taxation and regulation and that in force in neighbouring states, since the practice of cabotage has been permitted. But the contrast is marked in government policy and political attitudes to road freight transport and to the railway industry, and it is to be hoped that the current efficiency of road haulage and distribution will not become a political issue.

COMPETITION IN THE MARKET

Economic analysis must always start from the definition of the market concerned, and for this part of the transport industry the market is for the movement of goods. This of course means that road haulage and distribution are in the same market as rail freight, coastwise shipping, air freight and pipelines. In the interrelationship between the modes there is little danger of market failure, but the problem of regulatory failure does exist. Thus for some 40 years prior to 1989 the National Dock Labour Scheme reduced coastwise shipping to no more than a marginal competitor, an outstanding example of failure due to political pressure. More recently the industry's recovery has led to successful competition with road freight transport, and it may be argued that steps taken by central government to improve access to ports should be seen as a quid pro quo for damage done in the past. The same could apply to the support given to rail freight companies, since that business was virtually abandoned by British Rail prior to privatization. With or without such support, the rail freight companies have shown that they too can compete successfully with road haulage, although the potential for distribution is far more limited. Pipelines and air freight occupy market slots where road freight companies can do little to compete (though as we shall see the railway and pipeline industries are in much closer competition).

When all is said and done, though, the market for movement of goods is still distorted by the provision of the highway infrastructure at a price that is zero at the margin. Firms using every other mode of transport have to pay directly for the use of the track or the terminal facilities upon which they depend, and leaving externalities aside, the market would function beneficially and contribute to greater economies if the problem of track costs were to be dealt with.

CONCLUSION

Road freight transport and distribution together form an industry that has benefited since privatization from freedom from political intervention, and while the public at large may have some misperceptions and prejudices, operation has been subject to little more than the necessary quality control. Taxation and the externalities associated with the highways, and in particular with the motorways, are the most obvious areas where regulatory failure and the public choice issues arise, and the industry's trade associations engage in continuing debate where these are concerned. Government apart, the principal pressures on the process of the catallaxy come from the more extreme environmentalists and, less controversially, from the current concern for 'sustainable transport', which we shall consider in the final chapter of this book.

Questions for discussion

1. Which comes first, transport or logistics?
2. What is meant by the 'back-load problem'?
3. Why should firms operating only vehicles under 3.5 tonnes escape the need for an Operator's Licence?

10

Road passenger transport, including the private car

THE MARKET FOR MOVEMENT

In Chapter 7 we examined the 'neglected factor', the private car as a means of transport. The confusion that exists about its place in the market is illustrated in Table 10.1. If we look at the absolute figures and not the percentages we see the collapse of traffic in the bus and coach industry, and the steady demand for trains, but we also see the phenomenal growth of car traffic over the past 50 years. This growth is far greater than the fall in bus traffic, indicating that the car has greatly widened the market for movement in passenger terms. It is a very serious criticism of any industry if it is seen to have lost market share in an expanding market, but it is an even more serious criticism of both the bus industry and economic policy for transport that the market is seldom defined in this way. Throughout the field of passenger movement, transport policy has for far too long been public transport policy.

In the box on page 33 in Chapter 4, we looked at 'the strange decline of the British bus industry', which is what is illustrated in

Table 10.1 The neglected factor: passenger traffic in billion passenger kilometers and percentages (in italics)

Year	Buses and coaches		Cars, vans and taxis		Rail passenger services	
1952	92	*42*	58	*27*	28	*18*
1962	74	*25*	171	*57*	37	*12*
1972	60	*14*	327	*76*	34	*8*
1982	48	*10*	406	*81*	31	*6*
1992	43	*6*	583	*86*	38	*6*
1999	45	*6*	621	*85*	46	*6*

Source: Transport Statistics Great Britain 2000, The Stationery Office

Note: The trends shown here are often neglected. The figures for buses and coaches show the consequence of the bus industry's failure to recognize that the car had become its competitor until it was almost too late, but the growth in car use by far eclipsed the fall in bus traffic. Over this period the car offered increasingly greater accessibility to its users, who travelled more often and farther afield, making many millions of journeys that would not have been feasible by public transport. Railway traffic on the other hand remained remarkably stable, despite the closures of the later 1960s, and by the end of the period it was showing a significant increase.

Table 10.1. We identified market failure in the growth of a cartel which by the 1920s had come to dominate production, and also a regulatory failure, whereby the effect of the cartel on the market was strengthened. In this chapter we shall examine the outcome of these failures in more depth, but first we need to survey the impact of the private car on the market for movement. When we reflect upon the extent to which management in the bus industry seems to have been blind to what was going on we might perhaps speak rather of the strange suicide of the British bus industry when faced by the new competitor.

When the first cars were imported from France and Germany in the 1890s they were limited to 4 mph in the countryside and 2 mph in towns, with a man walking 20 yards ahead of them, regulations which were rapidly ignored. They were the preserve of the wealthy, and after the Prince of Wales had been seen riding in a car, Parliament progressively eased the regulations, so that from 1903 the speed limit was raised to 20 mph and cars had to be numbered and registered. Car production increased substantially, and grew even faster after 1918, but the car remained a relative luxury, owned by the better off. Prices fell however, and when smaller cars with lower running costs came onto the market in the 1930s they attracted middle-class buyers, while remaining on the whole a luxury, with car commuting still being relatively uncommon. From the 1950s however car ownership grew rapidly, as shown in Table 10.1, and car manufacture became an internationally competitive industry. With the expansion of ownership the car rapidly came to be seen as a middle-class necessity, while since the 1980s the growing second-hand market has meant that it has become a working-class necessity too.

The effect of this on the market for movement was limited prior to the period of rapid growth which began in the 1950s. What we have seen since then has been a remarkable improvement in the quality of passenger transport, as the car has given its users increasing ease of access to their desired destinations. At the same time the cost of movement has decreased, not least because the input of the labour factor has been reduced. Since to drive a car involves no labour cost, and labour amounts to some 60 per cent of the total cost of bus operation, the car has a marked advantage. To improve the quality of any product while holding its price constant amounts to a cheapening, and to combine this with an actual lowering of price makes the cheapening effect still more marked.

In short, the consequence of the entry of the car (and the taxi) into the market for movement has been to offer a significantly wider choice of price and quality, because the car is not limited by the element of fixed-route provision that applies to buses and coaches and still more to trains and trams. The 1950s saw the removal of trams from British streets, but too often the buses continued to run on 'invisible tramlines', and the attitude of management to the change might almost be described in similar terms.

BACKGROUND AND ORGANIZATION

Public passenger transport by road goes back to the 11th century, when carriers' carts began to serve the growing market towns, and carried a few people with their goods. They were the ancestors of the country bus firm of today. But it was not until the Tudor Settlement and the end of the Civil War that travel became safe enough for the well-to-do, and coaches became available, so that it was no longer necessary to travel on horseback. But to own a coach was expensive, and around 1625 someone had the bright idea of 'plying for hire'. This means offering to carry paying passengers, which spreads the costs over more users, and thus reduces the unit cost and makes it possible to charge fares that more people can afford. These vehicles were called hackney coaches, and the taxis and hire cars of today have the same title. The hackneys plied for hire on the street, but then someone thought of running regularly over longer distances, with separate fares, and around 1650 the stage coach appeared, spreading the costs by operating over a set route at advertised times, usually with pre-booking. So the distinction between public transport and the private car goes back to the 17th century, although in those days you had to employ a coachman if you travelled in your own vehicle. That apart, the economics of road passenger transport has changed little, with the big difference that now you can drive your own car.

In 1829 a man called Shillibeer had the idea of combining plying for hire and regular operation, and introduced a new type of vehicle in London, which he called the omnibus. Horse-drawn omnibuses appeared in towns and cities everywhere, and provided some inter-urban and rural services as well, and since the costs of owning a coach remained high they were used by people of all classes.

Spreading costs over greater capacity was the secret of the tramway, which appeared in 1860. Although it was more expensive to operate, since the track had to be constructed, more passengers could be carried behind the same horses because of the reduced rolling resistance of the tramcar on rails compared with the omnibus on the road. Another step in the same direction came when tramways were mechanized, sometimes with steam haulage but mostly by electric traction, starting from 1885. Much more expensive again, the electric cars could carry up to twice the number of passengers, so that costs were spread still further and fares could be kept down. The tramways were usually built to serve areas of high population density, which could supply the demand, and the omnibuses continued to serve the better-off parts of cities and towns, especially after the motor bus had replaced the horse bus before and after the First World War.

Motor bus services, the first dating from 1898, spread rapidly after 1918 and covered the whole country within 10 years, with long-distance coach services growing even more quickly from 1925. Many councils which had acquired local tramways supplemented them with motor buses, and a few, such as Eastbourne as early as 1903, introduced motor bus services from the first. The rapid growth of the new industry during the 1920s was not matched by similar growth in the use of cars, which remained expensive to buy and maintain despite their lower labour costs. The bus and coach industry could spread because there were few regulations to control it, making it highly contestable, but while many small firms and one-man businesses appeared after 1919, by 1930 many of them had been sold to the so-called 'territorial' companies which had spread over the whole of the country, beginning in 1916. In 1931 a system of licensing was introduced (see the box on page 108), which severely reduced contestability, and led to still more sales of this kind. The route monopolies that the new system provided could only discourage innovation and growth, just as the private car was becoming more widely available to the middle classes.

The Transport Act 1947, which nationalized the railways and part of road haulage, among other provisions, provided for the compulsory acquisition of bus and coach companies and the formation of Area Boards to operate the services. This was abandoned after the change of government in 1951, but two of the three big ownership groups had sold their territorial companies to the state by then, and the third was to do so in 1968. The Transport Act 1968 transferred these services to the National Bus Company or the Scottish Bus Group, though several larger firms and a multitude of smaller ones remained independent, while the municipal bus fleets were not affected. But the same Act set up four Passenger Transport Authorities in the conurbations, increased to seven in 1972, under

CURTAILING CONTESTABILITY

The Road Traffic Act 1930, introduced through Parliament with no debate, and based on the Report of the Royal Commission on Transport of 1929–31, provided for three types of regulation for public service vehicles (PSVs). The first provided for safety regulation or quality control for all PSVs and their drivers and conductors, and while this inhibited contestability, we saw the need for this type of intervention in Chapter 4. The second required a 'road service licence' to be held by any operator of stage carriage (local) or express carriage (longer distance) services. While existing operators largely held 'grandfather rights', the holder of such a licence could effectively ban any newcomer seeking to compete. (A third category was provided for 'contract carriage services', where it was forbidden to advertise the service or to charge separate fares.) The road service licence was a form of quantity control, introducing a local monopoly on each of the routes concerned. The third type of intervention, price control, was permitted for stage and express carriage services, and was quickly enforced on them all. The overall effect was to reduce contestability to a minimum, which led to the further consolidation of ownership of the industry around the municipalities and the territorial operators. The Royal Commission had recommended quantity control to deal with what it called 'wasteful' competition, but there were problems in the 1920s when drivers raced to get to the waiting passengers. Quality control could have dealt with that, without undermining the market.

which Passenger Transport Executives (PTEs) acquired the municipal fleets within their area and took over the services of the territorial companies concerned, either by compulsory acquisition or by directing their operations. Within these areas contestability disappeared.

For 25 years after the Second World War the bus industry lost business steadily, and by the start of the 1980s there was significant subsidy from public funds, almost all of it in the conurbations, where demand is most concentrated and the need for such intervention was least. As we shall see, the successful operation of bus and coach services was hampered by a disastrous misunderstanding of the industry's cost structure, but the regulatory system (see the box on page 110) had the effect of making managers think that their competitors were other bus companies, whose attempts to improve services they should fight off, whereas from 1950 onward car ownership soared, and the private car, no longer a luxury, was their real competitor. No attempt was made to meet this competition by effective marketing, and the control of fares introduced in 1931 prevented the industry from competing in terms of price and quality.

The Transport Acts of 1980 and 1985 (see the box on page 110) set out to deregulate and privatize the industry. Under this Act, the PTEs' bus fleets were in due course sold to private companies, and most of the municipal business were sold also. At the same time the industry was brought under the control of the Office of Fair Trading, to ensure that the renewed process of consolidation did not lead to nationwide ownership. The outcome has been the appearance of five major ownership groups, whose subsidiaries dominate the market and avoid mutual competition, along with a few independent territorial companies and a great many smaller firms. Contestability exists in principle, but the market power of the larger firms means that it is tolerated mainly at the edges, where the threat of smaller competitors encourages the larger companies to maintain efficiency and effectiveness.

The 1980 and 1985 Acts did not apply in London, where the bus business of London Transport was privatized, by way of franchise (see box on page 110), but in no way deregulated. As we shall find in Part Three, marketing is essential for the efficiency of bus operation, but the London bus companies have no freedom to engage in any marketing activity on their own account. However the provincial companies, with their increased freedom, have taken a long time to develop commercial expertise, marketing management, or price competition.

DEREGULATION IN 1985 – OR WAS IT MORE REGULATION INSTEAD?

The Transport Act 1980 took some cautious steps by way of removing the barriers contained in the Road Traffic Act 1930 (see box on page 108), setting up 'trial areas' with open competition for bus services. Little was learnt from them, but the Act removed the need for a road service licence for long-distance coach services, and ended control of fares throughout the industry. Pricing and costing policies among bus companies (most of them still nationalized) did not change. The Act of 1985 went further, ending the road service licence system and thus opening the industry to competition. As if the government could not trust this to work unchecked, it was made necessary to register the intention to provide a service, giving 42 days' notice, and to give similar notice of major changes or of the intention to withdraw the service. The operator was required to register the route and frequency and the size of bus that was to be used. This will be seen to seriously limit contestability. In fact, the 1985 Act introduced a number of new limitations on the market process, so that the bus industry was subject to more regulation afterward, not less. In addition there is evidence that regulatory failure further limits the benefits of a free and competitive market.

Recent legislation, though, has opened a way for the PTEs to regain their operating powers by way of franchise. This would provide for local authorities and PTEs to invite tenders to run bus services in their areas in accordance with the terms of the franchise. Sometimes called 'competing for the market', in place of competition in the market, it would in fact be competing for a monopoly. This is a 'monopoly' of bus services, of course, and not of the market for movement, where the private car is not going to be so easy to control.

COSTING AND PRICING

In Chapter 2 we saw the importance of understanding the costs involved in providing transport services, and how it is necessary to understand the significance of the marginal, or inescapable costs, the ones that you may have to incur anyway, such that any revenue that can come from running a service is worth having. There is an example of this in the box on page 15, and it is comparable to the back-load problem which we examined in Chapter 9. Small firms close to the market are well aware of it. Some coach operators (like many hauliers) have an idea of what each vehicle needs to earn per day, and where possible, prices are set to reflect this. (The problem of pressure on contract pricing we shall return to in Part Two, Chapter 12.)

A coach proprietor knows that 'getting the price (and quality) wrong', meaning wrong for the customer, can lead to the loss of valuable contracts, which is one reason these firms tend to stay small. The larger bus businesses have had to learn the lesson the hard way, because for them the loss or gain of a few passengers here or there does not show up in the profit and loss account. Because for 50 years their prices were controlled and they were unable to react to the market, they calculated their costs and revenue in terms of a rate per mile, and their test was how far average revenue compared with average cost on such a measure. Now it is clearly true that for the firm to stay in business, average revenue per mile must exceed average cost per mile, and by a margin sufficient to provide a return on capital and an element of profit for the entrepreneur, but to neglect the contribution of mileage that earns less than average cost, but contributes an element over and above the inescapable costs concerned, is to misunderstand the importance of spreading fixed costs over a greater quantity of output, thereby holding unit costs down and enabling prices to be related to 'what the market will bear'.

What we have called 'the strange suicide of the bus industry' followed from this misunderstanding of costs, but the average cost/average revenue measure was encouraged by the licensing system described in the box on page 108, and by the price control that was practised by the regional Traffic Commissioners where stage or express carriage services were concerned. (There was no price control in the area of contract carriage, so that the coaching trade was able to pursue the objectives of the small business which we have described above.) The road service licensing process encouraged bus operators to magnify their 'loss-making' mileage in order to object successfully to newcomers, and thus was done by comparing average revenue and average costs per mile, and claiming that all mileage earning less than average revenue was being operated at a loss. In this they ignored the contributory revenue that flows from mileage that earns enough to cover its 'out-of-pocket' (inescapable) costs, and thus contribute to overheads.

So long as the private car was not a serious competitor and income was reasonably steady this form of costing, while indefensible, had relatively little effect. There is evidence that managers before 1939 were aware of the true measure of financial success, though already it was coming to be seen that to magnify 'losses' was good tactics in the licensing system, and good public relations as well. The process began to undermine the financial health of the industry after the 1950s, as the market took in the newly effective competition provided by the use of the private car. First in the rural areas, but increasingly in the suburbs, and eventually in the area of concentrated demand in towns and cities, the average revenue per mile for the bus services tended to decline, while costs tended to rise, following increases in fuel tax each year and union pressure for higher wages. Using the average figures, the bus companies, increasingly state-owned after 1947, responded by cutting mileage.

The process was all too often self-defeating. Services, sections of route or timings were tested and found to be 'making a loss'. Mileage that could well have been contributing net revenue was cut, using average cost data applying to the whole company, and for the previous year's trading. The traffic concerned slipped away unnoticed, while demand for the private car increased. The outcome was to boost average cost per mile by the need to spread overhead costs over a reduced mileage, so that the next year's figures were even worse, and another tranche of mileage was cut. It was not a process that could go on for ever, but it came in due course to be used as an argument for subsidy.

In addition to this drastic distortion of the market, the industry after 1950 was subject to rigid price control similar to that which had been imposed on the railways from the late 19th century, but with even less flexibility. Using somewhat uncertain powers from the Road Traffic Act 1930, the Traffic Commissioners imposed a standard rate per mile on bus services, and while these varied to some extent from area to area, reflecting established differences of operating cost and of the level of demand, they denied any degree of market-based pricing (see the box below). Some small firms that had a 'monopoly' over a route were allowed to charge lower fares, but the principle remained that the same rate per mile was to apply to every passenger's journey. In the retail trade it is not the practice to expect the same rate of return from every line of goods in the store, or in the corner shop, but such discrimination was forbidden where bus and coach services were concerned.

MARKETING BY PRICE PROHIBITED

In the early 1920s a small bus proprietor started a service that linked two market towns by way of a number of villages. One of the towns was bigger and more attractive to shoppers than the other, and the fares were set so as to be cheaper for people going to the smaller town, with the outcome that demand for the service was well balanced. In 1950 the Traffic Commissioners enforced a standard rate per mile on the licence, bringing the fares in each direction into line with each other. Demand fell in both directions as people felt they were being exploited, and revenue per mile fell with it.

The need to magnify what was described as loss-making mileage was removed when the road service licensing system was abandoned under the Transport Act 1985, after which, as we saw in the box on page 110, it was no longer possible to object to a newcomer's proposed service. It took some time before the consequences of this were fully recognized for purposes of costing and pricing, and certain PTEs that failed to recognized the change found the market flooded with smaller competitors, and criticized the idea of contestability as a result.

Costing is generally better understood in the bus industry today than it has been in the past, and marketing by price is increasingly common. The price differential described in the box on page 113 is not unknown today, if not always approved of by traditional managers. Price competition has kept fares down where smaller firms have taken advantage of their lower overhead costs to enter the market. In London, where marketing management is denied to the bus companies and fares are set by a public authority, the pressure is on to achieve economies. While the term 'season ticket' is rarely used today, the sale of multi-journey tickets and unlimited use passes has grown rapidly since price deregulation took place in 1950, often with the intention of retaining custom where on-street competition exists. Where PTEs have introduced travelcards available on the services of all public transport in their area, including railway and tram services, the purpose has generally been to discourage the use of the private car. Some problems arise regarding the allocation of revenue, and the cost of doing so, but the spread of smartcard ticketing should simplify this kind of promotion.

It is important to remember that the price charged by the company, the supplier – let us call it the fare – is a cost to the passenger, the consumer. And let us remember too that there is more to the bargain than the money price, for the customer judges any product in terms of the mix of price and quality. Here the market for movement can be distorted by the problem of perceived cost. While regular users of public transport should be well aware of the fare and the quality of the journey and may have some notion of what these would be on a different trip or by a different bus or train company, the non-user or car owner has little opportunity to acquire such knowledge. Yet where marketing, including marketing by price, has been directed at the potential market for a bus service, there have been remarkable examples of how people decide to leave the car at home. As we shall see in Part Three, the use of market research is essential if the problem of perceived cost is to be reduced or set aside. But before any progress can be made in marketing, all public transport operators must recognize the further problem of generalized cost (see the box on page 115), which they should always allow for in a market that includes the private car.

THERE IS MORE TO COST THAN THE FARE

Almost everyone who has a journey to make would like, if it were possible, to get into a vehicle here, and get out there, now. Exceptions might be enthusiasts and people who enjoy driving, but in general, transport is a disutility, to say nothing of the external costs involved. But the disutility is not limited to the time involved and the price, for in addition to the fare, a journey by public transport may include all or some of these further 'costs': walking to the bus stop; waiting; walking and waiting again if it is necessary to change; and finally walking to the destination. Put these disadvantages along with the money price, and we have what is called generalized cost. Contrast this with the perceived cost of using a car, which appears to be cheaper and certainly avoids the walking and waiting, and the nature of the competitive market becomes plain.

The use of a car offers further benefits of a generalized kind. It offers privacy and ability to reach a number of destinations in one round trip. Car drivers tolerate systematic waste of time sitting in traffic queues, perhaps because they can listen to the radio, just as passengers on long-distance coach services may be offered the benefit of television. But the car has an apparent advantage over public transport, in terms of perceived cost, which is commonly underestimated by the user.

In seeking to satisfy the market, the commercial operator has to allow for mileage costs (fuel, lubrication and wear and tear), time costs (drivers' wages) and a range of overhead costs that must be covered from revenue. The car user is self-employed when driving, which is an advantage, but insurance and financial costs, such as hire purchase, are commonly regarded as overheads that can be ignored; indeed, once they have been incurred is it rational to maximize the advantage of car use. (It would be logical to allow for the opportunity cost of a garage, except that many car owners either use the street or use their domestic garage for various other purposes while keeping their car on the drive.) In the short run, which governs most decisions, even fuel may be seen as an overhead when there is a full tank.

Finally there is the problem of infrastructure cost, which applies to all road users, and which we examined in Chapter 8. There can be no doubt that the balance of advantage in the market for moving people would begin to shift from the use of the car to the use of public transport, by road or rail, if some form of point-based pricing were to be introduced. Without it the car will continue to have an advantage in perceived cost, as well as because of its extremely low labour cost, its genuine attractions notwithstanding.

ALLOCATIVE EFFICIENCY

Part of the argument for the Transport Acts of 1980 and 1985 was to improve the efficiency of the provision of bus and coach services. The coaching trade had retained contestability under the previous licensing system, and with it a competitive attitude to the market, which had kept firms small, and in that sector the market had tended, as unchecked it always does, to improve efficiency. The service operators, who by 1985 were predominantly in public ownership, existed in what was a virtually incontestable market (except for the competition of the car), and were given to the misunderstanding of costs and the control of prices that we have already examined. In addition there was a growing element of subsidy, and while this was often defended as wise use of public funds, its outcome is hard to measure, and it was inevitably subject to the problems analysed by public choice theory and the vote motive, which we examined in Chapter 5.

As a consequence of 'regulatory reform and restructuring', following from the Transport Act 1985, the bus and coach industry, since it has been moved largely into the private sector, has had to learn the importance of opportunity cost, which had been neglected to a considerable extent prior to that change. As we saw in Chapter 4, this is of central importance for the drive to allocative efficiency, and this, combined with the improved understanding of costs and prices that we have already observed, means that the industry today is in a much better state than it was before the 1985 Act. Contestability has increased, but as we saw in the box on page 110 it is still far from perfect. The balance of advantage still favours the private car, and since the choice of car travel cannot always be seen to tend to its efficient use, the market for movement of people is still a highly imperfect one.

We saw in Chapter 4 how the need to ensure safety requires a form of quality regulation that inevitably restricts contestability. For this purpose all firms operating public service vehicles have to hold a valid Operator's Licence, which is described in the box on page 95. Drivers are required to hold a PSV driver's licence, and drivers' working hours are limited. Failure to maintain safety standards can lead to the removal of some or all of the vehicles authorized by the licence, and failure to satisfy the regulations may lead to the suspension or removal of the licence, which puts the firm out of business. The Traffic Commissioner also has power to order a firm whose conduct is found wanting to repay an element of the rebate of duel duty that local service operators receive. Commissioners also penalize service operators for failures in timekeeping, despite the fact that these are frequently the result of road works and other circumstances beyond the operator's control. It is hard to see how this can tend to improve efficiency, and in any case it is to be supposed that to succeed in the market depends upon satisfying customers, who have been shown to rate reliability very highly in their evaluation of bus and train services. It would seem that the Traffic Commissioners fail to recognize that their decisions go beyond the standard definition of safety regulation, moving into the area of quantity control, and that the development of this intervention would justify analysis in the light of public choice theory.

Compared with this the private car is subject to minimum regulation, weakly enforced. As an industry it is very close to total contestability. Safety regulation consists of the 'MoT test', annually after the first three years from new, and the need to hold a valid driver's licence, for which a written and an on-road test must be passed. The requirement that a valid car licence must include any necessary MoT Test and a certificate of insurance, together with the driver's licence, forms a justifiable if inadequate safety regulation, but when these requirements are compared with the requirements for PSV operators and drivers they are negligible. Added to this, there is growing evidence that they are not complied with, and there is no limitation on drivers' hours. When we make the comparison between public and private transport, the conclusion must be that the market is heavily biased in favour of the car, and it cannot be argued that this tends to greater allocative efficiency.

CONSUMER EFFECTIVENESS

As the horse-drawn omnibus, the electric tram and then the motor bus were introduced they were an immediate success, attracting demand everywhere as they appeared on the streets. Although most people had to walk some distance to get to the bus or tram stop, this concentrated demand along the main corridors and meant better loading on the service. Poor standards of service in London led to the appearance of 'pirate' buses in 1919, but in 1924 they were made subject to quantity control, and most of them sold to the London 'combine'. The healthy market for public transport started to decline from 1950 as the car became increasingly available, and as we have seen the bus industry failed to recognize the new competition or to react to it other than by way of 'managed decline'. Demand fell rapidly and consistently, and by the 1980s the practice of maintaining operators by way of subsidy from public funds was beginning to undermine the working of the market, which if it had remained contestable might have been expected to seek out and satisfy passenger requirements. Since most bus operators by then were in public ownership, our understanding of public choice theory and the 'vote motive' will explain the shift away from the consumer's interest and toward the administrator and the local councillor, who increasingly distorted the market process.

The Transport Act 1985 banned the use of direct subsidy and, as privatization was carried through, made the bus companies profit-oriented, and therefore customer-oriented, in order to gain profits (see the box on page 110). One outcome has been to greatly reduce the distance of bus services from people's homes, while another has been the development of new services (many of which could have been justified 20 years ago). All too often the economic benefits of the market have taken a long time to reach the consumer, and there are parts of the country where too little change has been seen even yet. On the other hand there have been some outstanding examples of what can be done with good marketing management, bringing increasing demand and attracting customers who have the alternative of using the private car.

A FAILURE TO UNDERSTAND ECONOMICS

Commentators and members of the public may be heard to remark that 'businessmen put profits before passengers'. It is hard to see how such a stupid assumption could be made, since the only source of profit is the customer. It looks rather as if the period before privatization of the bus industry saw customers' interests neglected, or else why did passengers desert the industry in droves? The fact is that private businesses have a greater incentive to satisfy the consumer than self-regarding bureaucrats or vote-seeking politicians.

There is one problem that constrains the way the market tends to increased effectiveness, and that, strangely enough, is the impact of the Office of Fair Trading (OFT). So long as the monopolistic provisions of the Road Traffic Act 1930 remained in place, bus operators were exempt from this kind of control, but it seems that the OFT failed after 1985 to understand the economics of the industry, and some rather narrow assumptions led to regulations that have actually worked against the interest of the consumer. Thus where two firms run services on the same route they are not allowed to agree a joint timetable, which could in practice lead to improved frequencies. Prices have not been controlled since 1980, but the OFT is against any agreement to charge the same fares in such a situation, even though there is no attempt to prohibit retailers from doing so. The market, it can be assumed, is just as competitive on a bus route as it is on the high street, and it is even easier for a new competitor to appear.

The OFT is responsible for 'policing' the industry in another way, which is to limit the freedom of bus companies and ownership groups to merge. The trend to territorial dominance emerged as early as 1916, and the economies of scale that mark the industry have led to its reappearance since privatization in 1986. In Chapter 1 we contrasted the economics behind economies of scope, which can give improved efficiency within a business, but which come up against diseconomies of scale if they are pursued too enthusiastically. Among these diseconomies is the problem of rent-seeking, which we examined in Chapter 4, and when we look at the consequences of large scale for consumer satisfaction we should remember the saying 'the greatest monopoly profit is a quiet life'. Here, then, the OFT functions to protect the consumer from the consequences of yet further consolidation of ownership in the industry, which could be expected to weaken the effect of the market process in tending to optimum allocation of natural resources as well as the satisfaction of effective demand.

EXTERNALITIES AND THE ENVIRONMENT

The issues that we examined for road freight transport in Chapter 9 apply in much the same way to the bus and coach industry, but they are complicated by the place of the private car in the market. So far as environmental pollution is concerned, buses and coaches contribute far less than cars (see Table 10.2), and they are very much 'cleaner' on this count. There continues to be government pressure on car manufacturers to improve emissions standards, but the severity of congestion makes it difficult to achieve an acceptable level of input to the atmosphere. In terms of air pollution by trip, the number of passengers on a bus gives public transport a great advantage over the car, so we have here a further argument in favour of point-of-use road pricing (see Chapter 8). In the same way, the number of bus and coach accidents and fatalities is so small in comparison with the record of the private car that we may conclude that the environmental costs attributable to the bus and coach companies have been largely internalized.

Table 10.2 Air pollution by road transport: percentage of total emissions from road transport produced by each mode (1997 estimates)

Mode	Nitrogen oxides (NO_x)	Particles (PM10)	Carbon dioxide (CO_2)
Buses and coaches	7	8	5
Cars	54	27	61
All goods vehicles	40	55	34

Source: Confederation of Passenger Transport UK, *Facts 2000–2001.*

Note: Totals do not add up to 100% because of rounding. Nitrogen oxides and particles are the transport emissions of greatest concern for air pollution.

Government policy however has introduced a new kind of externality, which is in effect the denial of what may be called external benefits. The political phrase here is social exclusion, which means that some potential passengers are unable to use public transport (whether rail or road) either because they are disabled in some way or because their income is too low. It is true that the bus industry's record for customer care and customer friendliness has been very poor, and is now only improving in certain parts of the country. We shall return to this as an example of inferior marketing management in Part Three, but as economists we are entitled to sound a warning note. Attracting additional customers is generally taken to be desirable for successful trading, but to do it by subsidy, as has been government policy for some time, brings with it diseconomies, and the consequences of public choice theory. Some years ago British Rail introduced 'senior citizens' passes', offering reduced fares on off-peak services where there was empty capacity. Entirely without subsidy and just as sound marketing practice, the state-owned railway showed the way to deal with social exclusion, and then went on to offer similar promotions for students and families with young children. Elsewhere in the economy it is usual to find various price reductions designed to reflect demand; hairdressing is a common example. Such systems are easy and cheap to administer, but where public money is used for reduced or 'free' fares for the elderly there are significant operating costs. The amount of use has to be calculated by a form of occasional census, and the repayment of the fare to the operator has to be adjusted to remove the element of additional demand that has been created. Thus in order to spread an external benefit significant costs have to be internalized by a process which could well be avoided, while at the same time the intended social gain is extended to people whose incomes are sufficient for them to pay the commercial price. Where new investment, as in light rapid transit (LRT), allows for the expected use of 'senior citizens' passes', the implication is that the calculations include revenue from this kind of subsidy.

Bus companies and local authorities are spending considerable amounts of money to make travel easier for the elderly, the disabled and young mothers with small children, to list only three areas where problems of access are involved. That it should have taken so many years for these problems to be recognized forms a serious criticism of the ability of the bus industry to identify its product, and to cater for demand in the market. Here again we must allow for the fact that management for so long believed that the job was to run buses, not to satisfy customers. The car, on the other hand, offers the satisfaction that its owner desires and is prepared to pay for. The problem is that the car user seldom knows what the cost actually is.

Recently attention has turned to the provision of bus services outside busy cities and large towns, in which carryings are substantial and revenue strong, whereas each is weaker in the market towns and their catchment areas. Intervention by local authorities is proposed, apparently by way of some form of franchise. There are inescapable problems that arise when decisions are taken far from the market and applied by way of regulation, while there is also the potential of the 'vote motive' for further disturbance. It would seem that the problem has arisen from the 'territorial' structure of the bus industry, dating from 1916, whereby the larger firms have resisted the gradual transfer of services to smaller firms that are better able to provide them because of their lower overhead costs. It is a situation that has been developing steadily since the private car became a preferred alternative for people living in these 'out-lying territories', and it does the big bus companies no credit.

Alongside these problems there is the troubled area of rural bus services. There is no way in which the bus industry can offer the quality of service available from the use of the car, since demand is not concentrated as it is in towns and cities, and it was rural bus services that first felt the impact of competition from cars in the 1950s. A government committee examined the problem and reported in 1961, but little notice of the problem was taken for nearly 30 years. Since then rural bus operators have been offered subsidy, but largely in return for providing services designed by the local authority. Public officials, as we have seen, do not have the incentive to find out and satisfy actual demand, like the trader in the market, and this has led to marginally commercial services being withdrawn because of lost traffic, and subsidized services 'carrying fresh air'. The rural operators are invited to tender for the subsidy that goes with the chosen services, and then to re-tender after a period, so they have little incentive themselves to grow the market. Perhaps the best way to ensure that a basic level of services can be maintained with minimum subsidy is to give parish councils power to raise a rate and use the money to contract directly with local bus operators.

Economic analysis can provide little support for the existing system of subsidy, but when the cost of car use is brought into the calculation, the problem becomes even greater. It has been calculated that rural road users (including freight and public transport vehicles as well as cars) pay nearly seven times too much in terms of excess taxation (taxation over and above what is spent on the roads) when compared with the social and external costs that they create. Urban road users on the other hand are undercharged, to the extent that they are being subsidized by rural users: rural users are stated to be overcharged by 4.81 pence per kilometre, whereas urban central peak users are undercharged by 37.8 pence. If this imbalance were to be corrected the cost of car use would be reduced, although this would make the problem of providing for the non-car-owner appear even greater. If ever there was an example of regulatory failure it is here, but the way of restoring the benefits of the market is by no means plain.

TWO SPECIAL CASES

Buses and cars are not the only players in the market for passenger movement. There are also trains, light rapid transit (LRT) or trams, and taxis and hire cars. We shall analyse the 'railway problem' in the next chapter, so here we shall apply the template to trams and the taxis – omitting, admittedly, cycling and walking.

With the exception of the Blackpool line, electric tramways finally disappeared from British streets in 1960. The two factors that combined to undermine their efficiency are described in the box on page 125. When the Greater Manchester Passenger Transport Executive replaced two run-down suburban railway lines, and linked them using streets running through the centre of the city, with a spur providing a link between the two principal main line stations in Manchester, the result was a popular and successful hybrid form of transport, which has come to be called LRT.

Subsequently the Manchester lines have been extended, and new systems built in Sheffield, Croydon and the West Midlands, while others are under construction. As economists we should home in upon the allocative efficiency of the lines, not all of which have been successful financially, but it must be remembered that local government finance does not necessarily comply with the investment criteria of the private sector. Public investment in Britain must first be shown to promise an adequate rate of return (after discount), to satisfy the requirements of HM Treasury. The problem in terms of efficiency is that the Secretary of State is allowed to authorize construction that does not achieve this criterion, where it is stated to be in the public interest to do so. Since it is impossible to measure the 'public interest', it must be admitted that the investment can fail, as indeed it has already in certain areas.

Failures are not unknown in the private sector, where the outcome is to admit error, either by writing off the investment concerned or by way of bankruptcy, while if revenue more than covers operating costs, the service will be retained. It is open to question whether public money should be invested in projects where the decision is justified by so political a factor as the 'public interest', even after any potential external benefits have been allowed for. Finally, the losses that have been incurred on certain lines would suggest that their advantage in consumer effectiveness has been misjudged, with serious consequences in terms of opportunity cost.

THE DEATH OF THE TRAMWAYS

Many tramway systems were constructed by local authorities and private investors in order to provide an off-peak load for the local generating station, since there was then little demand for electricity other than for home, office and street lighting. As daytime demand grew during the 1930s most privately owned systems were converted to bus operation, but the tendency in the municipal sector was to continue to run the trams, or trolleybuses, at the reduced rate per unit of electricity that had been applied in past years.

One consequence of the nationalization of electricity generation and supply in 1946 was that these reduced rates were increased, often quite sharply, to reflect the better spread of demand, so that suddenly the system could no longer be justified financially, and buses were introduced in its stead. At the same time the growth of lower-density suburbs meant that demand was no longer concentrated so as to justify the high cost of tramways.

At the same time certain weaknesses in local government finance became apparent, since funds had not been set aside, as in a private business, for the replacement of the assets. Compared with the cost of buses there was no justification for the investment needed to replace tramway track and tramcars, where the few remaining suppliers were charging ever-increasing prices. It was these two factors, combined with the increased use of motor vehicles on streets carrying tram tracks, that led to the generally welcomed demise of the tram. The second factor seems likely in due course to affect today's LRT investment.

In terms of investment, the taxi is at the opposite end of the scale from LRT. The greater the cost of providing public transport, the greater is the requirement for concentrated demand to support it. In working busy corridors the taxi or hire car is in the same position as the private car, but its advantage lies in its ability to offer point-to-point trips over routes and at times where larger vehicles cannot find sufficient demand. If unregulated the taxi functions in a highly contestable market, but in many towns and cities the local authority, while maintaining safety regulation, used to restrict the number of taxi licences it was prepared to issue, creating a monopoly, which therefore justified the control of fares. While this was not opposed by the drivers, one consequence was to reduce effectiveness, while the value of a licence became a further charge on the trade, leading to pressure for fares to be increased. A substantial unsatisfied demand built up, and the efficiency of the market process became distorted. A consequence was the appearance of minicabs, unregistered cars seeking to enter the restricted market. In some cities (excluding London, where changes are now proposed), these traders were allowed, provided the journey was booked in advance. In due course provision for licensed hire cars was made available to provincial local authorities, while limitation of taxi licences was prohibited. The result is a highly artificial distinction, which has proved difficult to enforce.

It is plain that the market here is subject to serious regulatory failure, leading to uncertainties concerning safety alongside the abolition of quantity control. The market has become more contestable, but this is one of the few areas today where price control, for the traditional 'taxi', still exists. We have argued that this is one area in which price control is justified, since a cab driver can be in a strong monopolistic position if allowed to negotiate a price with a passenger on the street, for example late at night in bad weather. A heavy burden must lie upon the licensing authority when setting the price for a cab that is allowed to pick up passengers at the kerbside.

CONCLUSION

Even without its relationship with the railway, the market for moving passengers by road is highly complex, and subject to distortions arising from historical circumstances. The key weakness of economic policy is the continued absence of any form of pricing for the roads, which appear to the customer, whether this is a car owner or bus or coach company, to be 'free at the point of use'. There is thus no rationality in the decisions of car owners to drive or not to drive, while the phenomena of perceived and generalized costs make the decision process still more ineffective in letting the market tend to efficiency and effectiveness. The market process is still more complicated by the weakness of local government planning to allow for opportunity cost in arriving at allocative efficiency, and by the widespread examples of regulatory failure.

Questions for discussion

1. Why did the growth of car ownership and use take place unnoticed?
2. What do we mean by quantity regulation, as distinct from quality control?
3. What do we mean by 'the coaching trade'?

11

The railway problem

UTILITY OR PUBLIC GOOD

Railways play a part, if not a large one, in each of the two markets we have examined – the movement of people and the movement of goods. Why then do we have a separate chapter for them? The answer is given in the title of this chapter. The 'railway problem' arises from a widespread refusal to accept that railways are just another industry, and an assumption that they are somehow exempt from the principles of economics.

There are some who appear to claim that the product of railway transport is a public good, something that must be open or available to all, such as law and order, or access to public parks and monuments. They argue for 'fares free' transport (and on buses, too), with all costs paid for from taxation. Given the small proportion of the population that travels by train, this would be manifestly unfair, and where it has been tried it has proved to be unworkable. Others claim that railways (and buses) are a public utility, though this seldom extends to the movement of freight, and never to the use of cars. Other examples are said to be the provision of gas, water and electricity, which, with railways, used to be thought of as natural monopolies, unsuited for private enterprise and best provided by a public authority. In recent years it has been shown that competition can be introduced into all these industries, to the benefit of the consumer, which is why they have been privatized, with a regulator in each case to see that the new situation is not abused. But the inclusion of railways in this programme is rather different, because railways have always had to function in the wider market for movement. Thus among the arguments for privatization and some forms of deregulation the most powerful is to recognize the place of the market in promoting allocative efficiency.

There is a special case, though, which complicates the problem, and this is the contribution of railways to urban movement. In Greater London the railway and other modes together meet the shortage of land which we discussed in Chapter 6. The expansion of track in the 20th century led to the spread of suburban housing, yet the growth of commuter demand that followed has proved difficult to provide for. Subsidy does little more than to shift the problem to the taxpayer, but the normal relationship between supply and demand has fallen apart. The cause of this problem is the lack of an effective market for land. New investment in railways increases the value of the land through which they run, and this has been the source of substantial enrichment for landowners in urban areas where land is scarce. Taxation of land has been advocated for more than a century, and it opens the possibility of a return to the market for urban railways and the London tubes.

BACKGROUND AND ORGANIZATION

It seems to have been something of an accident of history that brought about the use of steel rails for steam traction to run on. The alternative that was being considered when the Liverpool and Manchester Railway was opened in 1835 was the provision of stone roads by a company that would operate its own vehicles and charge tolls for others to use the track. The problem we have today, of trying to promote competition on the rails (as required by the European Commission), would not have arisen.

The railway companies had to go to Parliament for authority to raise the capital they needed to build their lines, and for the powers of compulsory purchase of the land they required. Parliament was troubled by the accidents that were happening, and quality control was introduced quite quickly. The industry is fail-dangerous, and as we have seen, it is necessary to accept some limits to contestability on this account. Part of the railway problem is thus the interest taken by Parliament, and the intervention that has frequently followed, almost as if the government really wanted to run the railways itself. In 1844 an act was passed for the nationalization of any future lines, but since it did not apply to those already existing it had no effect. Gladstone again in 1864 proposed the acquisition by the government of the railway track, predating Railtrack by some 130 years, but nothing was done. The safety regulation continued to be strengthened, but by the middle of the 19th century the railways were starting to be seen as a monopoly. Complaints from trade and industry about unfair discrimination between customers led to intervention in the fares and freight rates that the companies were allowed to charge, and by the end of the century the rates were very much under the control of the Board of Trade. The last new main line to be built, the Great Central, opened in 1899, was a very disappointing investment, and from then on the combination of railway companies was seen to be inevitable.

After the First World War the government considered taking the railways into state ownership, but instead it was decided to merge them into four groups, known as the four main lines. They were made subject to still greater commercial regulation under the new Ministry of Transport, which hampered their freedom to compete with the new development of motor transport, and in addition they were 'common carriers' at law, and had to accept whatever goods traffic they were asked to carry, which gave their road haulage competitors a further advantage. By 1939 they were in financial difficulties, and no one was surprised when the post-war Labour government nationalized them in 1947. To start with they were part of the British Transport Commission (BTC), as the Railway Executive, but this did not stop them losing goods traffic to the Road Transport Executive, the nationalized road haulage sector. When the BTC was wound up in 1962 the railway business came under the British Railways Board (BRB), but it still suffered from the lack of new investment, a problem that is with it's successors today.

We do not know what might have happened in a private enterprise scenario, with or without state control of freight rates and fares, but the economics of the industry were severely distorted throughout the period of state ownership. Under Dr (later Lord) Beeching a great deal of mileage was closed, and there is no doubt that if this had commenced in the 1930s, so that the railways could concentrate on what they do best (moving large loads over long distances or at high levels of frequency) there would have been less of a political problem. Without the 'Beeching reforms', whether conducted by Beeching or someone else, the railways could well have collapsed in the way that they did in the United States. But the BRB did not have the freedom of action of a company board in the private sector, and was never certain where funds were coming from for capital investment, while political intervention (such as being forbidden to raise fares ahead of a general election) was not unknown. Too much depended upon what HM Treasury decided that BRB could be given, and as this was always an uncertain quantity the Board found it hard to plan forward. Although new investment had to be justified by an expected rate of return of 8 per cent after discount, the vagaries of funding did not make for efficiency in allocative terms.

One consequence of this was the preponderance of engineering over commercial management, and a tendency for managers to see their function as 'running trains', irrespective of what they carried, and not of maximizing the satisfaction of their customers. Substantial reorganization in the 1980s greatly improved this, and the operating subsidy had been drastically reduced, but the uncertainties of funding continued. The idea of returning the railways to private enterprise was inevitably controversial and highly political, but to return the industry to the market – the market for movement – was supported by a number of economists. Subsequent problems and failures seem to have followed from the decision to transfer the infrastructure to a separate organization, Railtrack, which was then privatized without strengthening the powers of the regulator. We discussed the issues concerned in Chapter 4.

COSTING AND PRICING

Enough has been said to show that the railways have inherited a history of price control, and it is to be remembered that freedom to set your own prices is central to freedom to manage, and to any serious marketing management. Understanding of railway costs had been frustrated for many years, so long as prices were set by the state, but after 1951 when the new Traffic Costing Service was set up there were great improvements. These did not always imply effective pricing, even after the statutory control of fares and charges had been abolished, and by the late 1980s the railways' share of the market for movement of goods appeared to be being phased out.

Today there are two approaches to the subject: costing and pricing by Railtrack and its successor, Network Rail (NR), and costing and pricing by the operating companies, which itself depends upon the policy of the track authority. The freight operating companies (FOCs), which are independent private companies, have complete freedom in pricing, but must be affected by NR's costs in addition to their own. The train operating companies (TOCs) are franchised, and since train fares are politically sensitive the Strategic Rail Authority (SRA) and the Rail Regulator are each concerned with the subject, limiting the freedom of the TOCs to respond to the market. There remains direct subsidy by government to the FOCs, to encourage the movement of traffic from road to rail, and the subsidy provided by the Passenger Transport Executives to the TOCs that operate train services in their area. Rail's share of the market is of course distorted by the absence of taxation on its diesel oil.

It is sometimes argued that railways by the nature of the industry can never cover their costs from charges in the market, and this is seen to justify state ownership or at the least state subsidy, and therefore state control. The economist will not that easily give up the argument that transport is best provided in an open market: a market for movement, within which the railway is just another player. The problem arises from history, and we have seen how government intervention in the 19th century led to price controls which lasted until 1962. Add to this the financial problems associated with the policies of HM Treasury, and the general neglect of the railways from 1945 to the present, and it should be no surprise that costs and prices became progressively unrelated. The result is the situation today, where rates and charges are too low to provide the income needed to balance the problem, but the necessary increase is politically unacceptable. We see how serious has been the regulatory failure that has led to the problems of today. But to argue that railways cannot function in an open market does not hold good on this analysis.

RAILWAYS AND THE USE OF LAND

We saw in Chapter 6 that the provision of transport has to compete for the use of land with other productive functions in such a way as to make its essential contribution to the satisfaction of community and industrial requirements while allowing for the relative scarcity of land and its opportunity costs. In Chapter 8 we looked at the central problems of infrastructure investment and pricing, which are, first, the lack of any balance sheet for the highways, and second, the absence of any pricing system for their use. It is this which makes comparisons of the efficiency of rail and road transport problematic, and it provides no formula for assessing the optimum use of the factor of land. Perversely it underlies the emotive arguments both for and against the construction of new railways or the retention of existing but under-used lines.

Throughout the 19th century railway companies had to use a good part of the capital that they were able to raise to pay for the land they required, and often at inflated prices. Much of the construction of largely unremunerative branch lines in the last quarter of the century (see the box on page 135) could have provided no return on the capital invested in land. With nationalization in 1947 the Railway Executive came into possession of what was called the largest and narrowest estate in the country, but the subsequent financial failure of the railway undertaking, and the arguments concerning the railway's future, means that the yield on this asset ranked very low in debate and discussion.

THE MARGINAL LINES

The final decades of the 19th century saw the railway companies under pressure from railway users to come under greater public control, their admitted economic power being interpreted as monopoly. Statutes in 1888 and 1884 gave powers to the Board of Trade and the Railway and Canal Commission to control their rates and to classify their freight carryings. This came at the same time as costs were rising, putting the companies under some pressure. Less formally perhaps, the companies were expected as a public duty to build new branch lines or to take over others that had been built by smaller firms, and that had never made much by way of profit. Within 20 years the demand for these services had been undermined by the growth of road freight and passenger transport, and by the 1930s they were already beginning to be closed. While others remained in operation until the Beeching reforms of the 1960s, most of them had contributed an outright loss virtually from their construction, calling into question the opportunity cost involved in acquiring the necessary land. Little was heard of this issue during the opposition to the 'Beeching closures'.

The railway has been around for so long that it is generally taken without question to be essential, so much so that in some European countries the national system operates with substantial subsidy from taxation. It may seem difficult to imagine inland transport without the railways, but it is still possible to ask the question, what if they had never happened? Steam-powered vehicles were being developed for use on roads for some 30 years before the opening of the Liverpool and Manchester Railway. Thomas Telford, the great engineer responsible for building the highway from Holyhead to London, was sceptical concerning railway investment, and he was one of those who sought to float the London, Liverpool and Holyhead Steam Coach and Road Company, which would have provided a paved carriageway over which it would have operated its own vehicles, and charged tolls for others to do so. The immediate financial success of the Liverpool and Manchester diverted investment into the new railways, while landowners sought to stifle the use of steam on roads for another 60 years, and today we so easily assume that there was no alternative to the railway age.

It is of interest to economists that Telford is reported to have observed, at the opening of the Liverpool and Manchester Railway on 15 September 1830, that the amount of traffic that could be carried on the railway, compared to the potential of the highway, meant that the cost of land for railway building offered a lower return on investment. In other words, the opportunity cost of land for railways was unduly high. In support of his argument, Telford raised an issue that is still relevant today, which is the limit to the volume of traffic that can be carried by rail imposed by the length of time when there can be no movement. Little work has been done on the comparisons involved, but the opportunity costs involved in new investment today should take the optimum use of land into account, whether in regard to new main lines or to the reopening of rural railways closed because of minimal demand.

Any section of rail track is incapable of maximizing its potential user value, and thus its return on investment, to the level that would be represented by continual running of stock, since the trains have to leave gaps between them for safety. Ironically, to run the trains slower makes for greater use of the track. At one extreme commuter lines carry passengers up to the safety limit, but in one direction only, and for a limited part of the day. (See the box on page 137.) The same problem of 'the peak' applies to most long-haul railways, while for them the unused period of time must be greater, because of the speed of the trains. At the opposite extreme, to run four or five trains on weekdays on a rural railway is difficult to justify in financial terms, since the line is unused during the greater part of its life. (See the box on page 137.) The argument in favour of rail travel that relates to unquantifiable social benefits might best be solved by inviting residents and business along the lines to contribute the necessary subsidy.

THE COMMUTER LINES

When the major railway companies built their main lines, the cities that they served were still compact, their area indicated by the spread of the horse-bus services that grew up after 1829, starting in London and Manchester. There was thus no scarcity of land in the suburban areas on the scale that we are familiar with today. To give one example of what followed, the directors of the London and North Western Railway doubled their tracks into Euston, and provided intermediate stations lacking on the main line. Later the Metropolitan Railway set out to capture the growth in land values by promoting 'Metroland', while in the 1930s the Southern Railway electrified its suburban lines and built new ones; there, too, property development followed on a large scale, though the railway company made no gains from it. Similar developments in all the great cities had the same effect, in benefiting landowners, while at the same time creating 'the problem of the peak', which limited the earning power of the new investment to a few hours in each direction each weekday. Thus the railway companies of the 19th and 20th centuries in effect created the problem of suburbia and the overcrowding that presents such a problem today.

A busy motorway filled with traffic often contrasts with the main line railway that runs for a few miles beside it, and appears to be empty most of the time. To offset this, it must be remembered that each train has the potential to move a greater volume of traffic than can the number of trucks, coaches and single-occupant cars that occupies a similar space. This familiar phenomenon deserves attention, but it is difficult to compare the efficiency of the investment concerned, because of the lack of any balance sheet for the motorway. It is of equal importance to recognize that many motorways are themselves empty for a great part of their lives, as a result of mistaken investment. The problem lies at the heart of the economics of transport, but there seems to be little political will to address it, perhaps because of the emotional involvement we observe among supporters of both railway and highway movement.

Finally, in addition to the problems of relative return on investment, the railway problem in Britain is complicated by the consequences of price control over a period of more than a century, as well as by the distortions that marked the period of public ownership, when the railways were no longer managed as a commercial enterprise. What entrepreneurial drive their managers had, and it was not lacking, was repressed by the risk-averse policies of HM Treasury as well as direct political intervention. These problems have not departed, but perhaps their most serious consequence has been that prices rise, or fall, according to the costs of operation and the contemporary economic climate. It is worth comparing the railway industry with the retail trade, and to ask what could have happened to the supermarket chains and the 'anchor stores' if their management had been subject to the same mixture of neglect and intervention from which the railways have suffered, none of it justified in economic principle.

This outline analysis of the railway problem touches upon one thing that must concern the economist, which may be expressed by the statement, or belief, that 'railways are a good thing'. Safety apart, standards of quality are expected by passengers of the Train Operating Companies that do not seem to apply to airlines or to the use of the private car. While it is recognized that the way rail privatization was designed has led to many of the weaknesses of the situation today, the pursuit of economic efficiency – the optimum distribution of scarce resources – requires the railway industry to be treated like any other. In economic terms, rail transport should be able to justify itself; but this will be difficult to achieve as long as the highways are regarded as 'something else'.

ALLOCATIVE EFFICIENCY AND CONSUMER EFFECTIVENESS

Improvement in these aspects of rail transport was the principal objective of privatization. It seems to have been achieved in the case of freight traffic, although even there conflict with the growth of passenger demand and the problems suffered by Railtrack have restricted the tendency to improvement. A great part of the problem arises from the neglect of rail transport, passenger or freight, by governments of both parties since 1945. Readers should apply the principles from Part One and come to their own conclusions on what is still a highly political subject, though the distortions that exist make such an analysis very problematic.

What appears to be plain is that the growth of demand, both from passengers and freight customers, has overcome the process of privatization, at the same time as what must be taken to be mismanagement by Railtrack plc has led to increased congestion on the railway. Several serious accidents have undermined public confidence, and awoken the call from those who see the industry as a 'utility' to return it to state control if not state ownership, which has now been achieved. But this is to ignore the problems of public choice theory and the 'vote motive', which always tend to constrain both efficiency and effectiveness. The railway problem does not look as if it will go away.

EXTERNALITIES AND THE ENVIRONMENT

Electric traction may reduce the volume of environmental pollution, but it must be recognized that although electricity may appear to be a 'clean' fuel, electricity generating stations are often burn fossil fuel and create pollution, so the use of electricity only puts the pollution further back in the production chain. It seems now that the reduced levels of emissions from modern diesel engines could start to shift the balance of advantage away from electric traction. Railway diesel has never been subject to fuel tax, thus reducing the internalization of pollution costs in contrast with road vehicles. Noise pollution, which at certain times and places can be substantial, is not very often remarked upon. There is some pressure for railways to accept regulation so as to reduce 'social exclusion', but the current high prices reflect high operating costs and the need to expand the service, so any intervention here would imply substantial provision of subsidy. Political issues like these must be set against the severe overcrowding on many suburban lines, and the readiness of passengers to pay high fares for many journeys by train.

CONCLUSION

The railway problem is a serious issue in economics, complicated by the political as well as the economic significance of the industry. Commercial intervention by government since the 1890s has left a tradition of control, which it is very hard to justify in economic terms, apart from safety regulation. As a result, the tendency of the market to encourage both efficiency and effectiveness is constrained, and the distortions that arise in the market, for the movement of people as well as for the movement of goods, have a knock-on effect greater than might be expected in terms of the small element of production that the railways contribute, at such cost. (Readers whose feelings for the railway may make it hard for them to accept this argument should reconsider it in terms of economics rather than emotions.)

Questions for discussion

1. Why are railways seen to be so important?
2. How can railways compete in the markets for movement?
3. What is the railway problem?

12

Transport and tourism

BACKGROUND AND ORGANIZATION

Travel for recreation and self-improvement is a very ancient pursuit, but for centuries it was reserved for the wealthy (or for military campaigns). In the 18th century the education of young men of rank in Britain often concluded by making the 'Grand Tour' of France, Germany, Switzerland and Italy, in the company of an older and usually scholarly tutor. In the first half of the 19th century, before the spread of railways in Europe, the market grew as the better-off became able to travel by diligence, a horse-drawn passenger vehicle which provided public transport between towns at less cost than the hire of a carriage. Journeys became easier to plan and to make as the railway network spread, and the contribution of tourists to the national economy came to be recognized. Tourists were almost always members of the middle or upper middle classes, but the demand was sufficient for pre-planned tours, with accommodation provided, to start to appear.

Tourism by this time was becoming an industry, and the growing demand was met by the construction of hotels, and of railways to mountain tops in Switzerland. Thus as an industry tourism depends upon two support functions, first, catering and hospitality, and second, transport. Each of them is a very ancient industry in its own right, and each provides for other categories of demand, while catering in turn has always been dependent upon goods transport to enable it to function. The later 19th century saw the growth of travel and tourism both to the traditional areas of Europe and to seaside towns and inland areas within the United Kingdom. Among the last places where stage coaches ran were south Devon and the Lake District.

The coming of the railway saw the development of mass tourism, with railway excursions at very low prices, starting already in the 1830s. The growth of this trade is associated with Thomas Cook, who organized his first trip in 1841. Demand was significant both out of and into London, while the citizens of Brighton deplored the excursion trains that brought down loads of cockneys, who were seen to spoil the town's middle-class image. The Great Exhibition of 1851 saw excursion trains from all parts of the country, catering for all classes of passenger, with extremely low fares justified by the scale of the demand. This form of tourism was dependent upon transport alone, but the middle classes continued to demand organized tours, with catering and hospitality included, and the 1920s saw the start of coach tourism, both at home and to the continent, with accommodation also provided. Only with the cheapening of air transport did the international mass tourism market develop. In Britain the market grew as increased wealth and the social changes that accompanied it made for rapid growth of demand, concentrated on parts of Europe known for sea, sand and sex. Inclusive tours could then be distinguished from inclusive holidays.

COSTS AND PRICES

There are many similarities between the economics of transport and the economics of catering and hospitality, none greater perhaps than the fact that for each, the product is consumed in the moment of production, or if not, then it is gone for ever, with consequential waste. (We shall return to this in Part Three.) The product of passenger transport by any mode, including the private car, is usually measured by passenger kilometers, while the product of a hotel is conventionally measured by bed nights, the number of bedrooms occupied in any period of 24 hours. The pressure to fill all available accommodation is great, leading to sophisticated pricing, which includes significant discounts for mass booking.

Where hotels and coach tour operators sell direct to the public they function in a primary market, whose contestability is subject only to external regulation, whether quality control for transport or quality control and land-use regulation for hotels and boarding houses. Many hotel and coach proprietors prefer to remain in this market, where they understand their costs and can set their own prices for their customers. We may call this an extended market for movement, but for the coach operator it is also a sector of that market. (For hoteliers too it is a sector of the catering market.) So long as pricing remains largely in the hands of the producers, whether in transport or hospitality, the economics remains straight-forward, but superimposed on these two industries there has grown up a kind of hybrid market, where the players are the tour operators.

Those tour operators who own or lease their aircraft, or operate their own fleets of coaches, normally buy in catering and hospitality, but other firms do not own any vehicles or aircraft, and must get the best rates they can from the transport operators. If we concentrate upon the coach industry in Britain (although the civil aviation industry has similar problems), we find that the fractured market gives rise to problems for the firms whose product they need to buy in. Mass tourism is a highly competitive industry, and profit margins are narrow, leading to heavy pressure to keep movement costs low. As well as some larger firms there are many 'tour operators', including newspapers and firms offering tours in specialist sectors of the market, and all these firms have overhead costs which must be met. This makes for an incentive to drive down the prices they pay to coach operators, whose margins are also likely to be tight. Many small firms undertake work at dangerously low rates in order to obtain turnover, despite constant explanation in the trade press of the dangers of accepting whatever work is available, and failing to bargain for better terms. In a sector of the industry containing so many small competitive firms it has never been easy to encourage membership of trade associations, while there is the Office of Fair Trading to take an interest in suspected price-setting, so the hybrid market may have the unsatisfactory outcome of lowering standards of safety.

Just what, then, is the market for tourism? Internationally, there is a major income for those who live in places where tourists want to go. Export tourism, the movement of people into a country, must be set against import tourism, which is the opposite, people going away to other countries. Within Britain each type is involved in the transport market, together with the movement of tourists and holidaymakers here at home. It is a very large market to try to define, but its implications for the market for movement, both freight and passenger, are of serious importance. Take for one example the problem of congestion, where every holiday period is marked by crowded motorways and train services. Consider the pressure upon 'tourist attractions', well expressed by a local authority official who said, 'The Lake District is full!' What do you do when cars and coaches fill all the available road space, defeating the very objective of the sightseeing tourist?

We have seen how tourism started as a privilege for the rich, and has become the mass tourism of today. Irony is always an aspect of truth, and no more so than in the saying, 'The explorer goes where no one has been before; the traveller goes where few people have been before; the tourist goes where everyone has been before.'

ALLOCATION AND EFFECTIVENESS

The two levels of the market make it difficult to assess the allocative efficiencies involved, but the pressure on the coaching trade to cut costs so as to obtain contracts at or below marginal levels of profit must be a matter for concern. This is a specialist sector of the market, and tour operators who own their own vehicles, as well as coach firms who operate their own tours, to a large extent escape the problem, while remaining in the same overall highly competitive market. Certainly the mass movement must be wasteful of resources, but the need for 'block bookings' of both accommodation and vehicles or aircraft seems to make this inevitable. Margins are tight throughout the tourism business, and from time to time reports of 'holidays from hell' indicate that effective customer satisfaction has its limits. The situation must give concern to the economist, but it is a matter not of market failure, but more basically of the relation between supply and demand in a very complex market.

EXTERNALITIES AND THE ENVIRONMENT

Transport makes tourism possible, and the growth of transport for tourism increases the problem of external costs that we examined in Chapter 10. Within Britain they are centred on the problem of track costs. Effective road-use pricing could have some effect on the peak problems of tourism, if only by increasing prices to a more rational level. It could also be the answer to the congestion problem so well illustrated by the statement, 'The Lake District is full'. It is here that the lack of balance between the private car and public transport appears as a crisis, with the additional problem of costs imposed on the local economy when local residents and traders have no freedom of movement over a significant part of the day. Distribution is central to efficiency in the catering and hospitality function of tourism, and congestion on this scale makes for inefficiency. Deliveries may of course be made in the early morning or the evening, but this increases labour costs, while the most convenient time for deliveries is the middle of the day, when hotel and boarding house guests are away from the premises, but when congestion costs are highest.

Damage to the environment arising from tourism is a further external cost that is far from being brought to book. 'The consumption of heritage' is a phrase used by students of tourism, and while this may seem strange it includes the effects of overuse on paths and trackways, even to the level of mountain tops, as well as the costs of maintaining publicly owned properties where no admission fee is charged. In the same way as the use of land for car parks this illustrates yet once more the problem of the car in the market for movement.

CONCLUSION

Leisure travel for tourism is part of a mass market that is embedded in today's society. The contribution of 'import tourism' and the demand at home are very significant elements in the prosperity of the community. We saw the effect of foot and mouth disease on both home and import markets, while the September 11 disaster struck at tourism worldwide. But for the United Kingdom the holiday market is the important sector where transport is both essential and problematic, while the economic outcomes remain to a large extent doubtful.

Questions for discussion

1. Who pays for carrying the tourists?
2. What is meant by 'export' and 'import' tourism?
3. What is meant by 'the consumption of heritage'?

Part three

The meaning of marketing

13

Efficiency, effectiveness and the marketing mix

MARKETING MANAGEMENT

Most people probably associate marketing with advertising and promotion, and this is not unknown within the transport industry itself. The result is that marketing gets to seem less important than engineering, finance or operational management, and its costs are seen to add nothing to the value of the product. But there is no point in producing something that customers do not want at the price on offer, so the corporate business of the firm can be called marketing management. This is how the economist analyses the business, for wasted output weakens efficiency and undermines the satisfaction of effective demand. In the next chapter we shall define the principles of good marketing, and then we shall apply them, again as a template, to see how efficient the modes of transport are on this analysis, and how much freedom they have to pursue the objectives of marketing.

Transport is a service industry, with the same problems and opportunities as catering, hairdressing, telecommunications and many other branches of business. The product of transport is a service, not something you can buy in a shop and take home, or have delivered to your factory. (But supermarkets came into existence to provide a service, and customers expect the same standards now when using trains or buses.) Unlike most goods, a service cannot be stockpiled. So every empty seat in a bus in service is production unsold and running to waste. Perishability is the keynote for production of services such as transport, and one statement should be remembered by everyone involved in the industry: in transport, production and marketing are inseparable. Manufacturers can carry stocks of their products, so they can still supply the market when there is a hold-up in production, but this is impossible for the service sector. A hairdresser in a slack period will have assistants sitting around, being paid despite making no contribution to income; a truck driver in a motorway queue is in the same situation. Some waste, though, is inevitable; in freight transport it gives rise to the 'back-load problem' (see Chapter 9), while buses and trains outside peak demand periods will have empty seats, and thus wasted seat-miles. (Good marketing, of course, will offer special fares to attract custom, because the costs involved in running the service will probably be inescapable.)

DISTINCTIVE CHARACTERISTICS OF SERVICES

There are four aspects of service provision, each of which is of importance for the transport firm. First there is perishability, which we have just described. Every unit of output, whether seat-miles or capacity tonne-miles, perishes in the moment of production. Economists do not like waste, because it tends to reduce allocative efficiency, and it is no escape to subsidize provision of a service. Paying bus firms to run virtually empty buses (see Chapter 10) is an example of this kind of waste, which has a measurable effect on the efficiency of the firm and thus of the economy. Roadworks and other traffic delays means vehicles standing idle, wasting fuel and delaying delivery. Car drivers may find an alternative route, but buses suffer from an incremental delay.

The second characteristic of services is their intangibility. You cannot get hold of the product of transport and assess its qualities before you decide whether or not to buy it. The producer must seek to build a reputation for quality, which can all too easily be lost. This is also related to inseparability, which emphasizes the relationship between the quality of the product and the ability of the seller, who for the transport industry may be defined as the sales staff; the booking clerk, the train crew or the courier, and finally the driver. Customer-friendly staff are essential to success in any service industry (bus drivers not least), while the provision of 'added value' in the distribution business means that truck drivers are just as important.

Finally there is heterogeneity, which is about the difficulty of providing a standard quality, which you would expect when buying tangible goods. Too many of the circumstances under which production takes place are beyond the power of the firm to control. In the railway, freight transport and bus or coach operation, probable yet unforeseeable interruptions can occur at any time. Poor depot management may lead to inappropriate vehicles being scheduled, but the customer cannot be expected to allow for quality failures, however they may arise.

DEMAND AND THE PRODUCT

There is a danger that the meaning of marketing may be lost in the jargon with which it is associated. If we go to the heart of the matter, we might express it this way:

> In transport, marketing means making sure that what we produce we can sell and that we sell what we produce, at a price that satisfies both user and seller.

That definition is not far from what we said about the meaning of economics at the beginning of this book, which shows how important marketing is to efficiency and effectiveness, which we discussed in Chapter 1. As for what the product is, we measure it in terms of seat miles or capacity tonne miles (see Chapter 1, page 6), and the (unattainable) objective of the industry is to sell them all, in the moment they are produced (as we have just seen). In Chapter 14 we shall examine the marketing mix in terms of the 'seven Ps' which together form the basis of the marketing concept. Here we shall concentrate on one of them, people, because no progress is possible without the concentrated attention of everyone in the business on the objective of marketing, which is very close to the survival of the firm. First, though, we must examine the realities of the market.

There is a generic demand (or 'need') for transport, which is expressed in the definition of the product, which we met in Chapter 1, as the safe arrival or delivery of passengers or goods. The cost of freight transport is a deficit for the logistics manager, justified only by the increased value of the items carried somewhere else. For almost all passengers the journey is more or less of a disutility, to be undertaken, again, because we want to be somewhere else. This is why product-driven businesses in the transport industry will always fail. Management and operational staff at every level need always to realize this, and must recognize the nature of the competition that they face (see the box).

ALTERNATIVES IN THE MARKET FOR MOVEMENT

For passengers who seek transport for access to satisfactions at some other place, the choice, varying with the length and convenience of the journey, lies between airlines, railways, light rapid transit, buses and coaches, taxis and hire cars, private cars either as driver or passenger, motor or pedal cycles, and walking. For freight customers there may be own-account vehicles, road hauliers, distribution companies and couriers, as well as railways, coastwise shipping, and to some extent freight airlines and pipelines. Whatever transport business you are in you must identify which of these market sectors you seek to serve and how effective the competition may be from other modes. But you must also allow for the ultimate competitor: telecommunications, which can replace the need for physical movement, whether for passengers or freight.

Product-driven management, which assumes that you have only to offer a service and customers will pay you to use it, has been shown all too often to fail. Characteristic of the railway and bus industries through most of the 20th century, it has never been the practice of the private car business or of road haulage and distribution, where managers must go out and get their trade. Within each mode of transport, variations in the market must be taken into account – in tourism, where they range from businesses sending senior staff by Concorde to the basic package holiday in Lanzarote; for railways, where elasticity of demand varies from the commuter to the day tripper; on the buses, whose clientele varies by social class and by time of day; and throughout the road and rail freight business, where everything turns upon managers' detailed insights into the requirements of a wide range of different types of customer.

OBSTACLES TO MARKETING

Ultimately successful marketing depends upon communication, within the firm and between the firm and the potential customers out there in the market, and this means understanding the product and understanding the market for it. It is something that any small business in a competitive market must undertake in order merely to survive. The coaching trade is notable for the small size of the typical firm, and this reflects the need to keep in close touch with customers in order to retain their orders. Here the proprietor or manager is practising marketing perhaps without even knowing it. Coach operators and small hauliers depend upon renewed orders, and the loss of a regular customer can mean going out of business. In railway and bus transport it is unlikely that management will know that it has started to lose custom until it is getting too late, which means it must undertake marketing research and market intelligence in order to know what is going on. At the same time it is far more dependent than coach transport upon well designed promotion, publicity and public relations, not to forget central and local government officials.

Much of this may seem strange to the general public, where transport is seen as something different from the retail trade. There are four false arguments frequently put forward, which we must dispose of here. The marketing of transport services is frequently assumed to be impossible, unnecessary, indecent and dangerous. Let us consider each of these in turn.

Marketing is impossible

This assumption is heard less often today than it has been in the past, as the commercialization of the formerly state-owned sectors of the industry has proceeded. 'Providing a service' was formerly seen to be the function of the transport undertaking, while questions as to its financial success were sidelined. Just to cover the costs of the operation is an objective that makes no sense in economics, and provides no way of measuring success in terms of either efficiency or the effective satisfaction of customer demand. For any transport business to succeed in these objectives, marketing is essential.

Marketing is unnecessary

This is the assumption that all an operator need do is to provide a service, and customers will find out about it and use it. 'The bus is its own advertisement' is a sadly inadequate slogan, if you do not know what people want of the service: its price, its quality, its frequency, even its destination. Where public subsidy is available, administrators may neglect the profitability that drives the private sector firm, by trying to second-guess these matters, but for the economist the signals to be read in the market must provide the information that determines the production of services that provide a return on the capital employed, and a profit to attract the innovator and the entrepreneur.

Marketing is indecent

Some people seem to believe that the promotion and selling of any commodity will make people buy it when they do not really want to. Anyone engaged in marketing will know the answer, in the slogan, 'You can make the customer buy the wrong product – once!' What marketing can and does achieve is to make the public aware of the choices that are available, but eventually the buyer will decide what is the best available mix of price and quality.

Marketing is dangerous

This, perhaps surprisingly, is the only respectable criticism of the marketing of transport services. As we saw in Chapter 4, the industry is fail-dangerous, and even the best qualified engineer cannot judge from the track or the roadside just how safe is the train or bus that invites public use. It is true that unscrupulous firms may be tempted to take 'short cuts' over maintenance of equipment or in recruiting engineers and operative staff, and this is why quality regulation is needed in all sectors of the industry. But cutting corners is not the objective of marketing management, which recognizes that only a safe and reliable product will sell. It is the suitability of the product that must concentrate the mind of management, and that is what marketing is about.

To the extent that these beliefs about marketing are held by the general public, they are plainly far from the truth, at least so far as quality regulation is in place. What marketing management seeks is, in equally simple terms, the satisfaction of the customer and the survival of the firm. This is not to assume that every transport business is structured in this way. As we shall see, to have a marketing department is not enough.

PRACTICAL MARKETING

The specialist areas of marketing, each of which contribute to the success of the business in practice, are market intelligence, marketing research, marketing communications and promotion. In practice they will vary in their application in the different branches of transport and distribution, but much can be learnt from examining their principles.

Market intelligence is the basic requirement for good marketing management. It consists of gathering all the information feasible concerning the market in which we are selling our services. It is future-oriented and its function is to scan five areas of the environment within which the firm is engaged. These are:

- modal and intermodal competition;
- changes in the state of the economy;
- social and cultural trends;
- attitudes in government and politics;
- technological developments.

No one source can provide all this information, so even in a small firm the managers need to track these areas systematically, in so far as each of them is central to the future of the business. In the larger firm it is not enough to leave it to the directors; journals and magazines should be circulated, in the hope that managers are not too busy to study them, and debate and discussion should be encouraged. The key question is 'What if?': what could be the consequences of change under each of these headings?

In support of these concerns, a function of market intelligence is to gather data regarding local changes in the market, the actual performance of the firm, and what is happening to the competition, all of which is essential for the design of a promotion campaign. This was well illustrated by the Duke of Wellington when he said, 'All the business of war, and indeed all the business of life, is to endeavour to find out what you don't know by what you do; that's what I called 'guessing what was on the other side of the hill'.'

Marketing research is often confused with 'marketing'. We think of an interviewer with a clipboard in the high street and call that 'market research'. That indeed is what it is, but the wider definition that we use here includes both deeper and wider analysis. The use of market research projects must be controlled, because the data may already exist from market intelligence. Such projects are on the other hand fundamental to many promotion exercises, as well as to the analysis of schemes for investment. But the more sophisticated programmes can be very expensive, and many transport firms will find it pays to make use of a reputable consultancy to undertake anything of this kind in depth. What is important is for managers and directors to be thinking about the firm's needs, and spotting the cases where expenditure on properly designed research is to be preferred to guesswork.

Marketing communications includes much more than advertising. It is about getting the product known, to both new and prospective customers, and making sure that new developments arising from marketing research and technical progress are brought before the public effectively. What we have to communicate to the market comes under two heads: material to build a positive image, and hard information about the product.

Both processes will be supported by the use of a consistent house style. This must run through all uses of the media, right through publicity material to such things as the company's stationery, and it is here that the vehicle on the road is its own advertisement. The train operating companies have realized this, but practices vary in the bus industry, where the use of a national image may not be better than the encouragement of local loyalties, while route branding may encourage the customer to see the vehicle as 'my bus'. Road freight and distribution firms are open to criticism for weak house style, with many of them logging on to the word 'logistics' with little thought given to what it means.

As part of the process, advertising is essential. Without it, survival can never be assured. The problem is finding a justification for the expense. It is well said that half the money spent on advertising is wasted; unfortunately there is no way of finding out which half. Do-it-yourself stores, supermarkets and the motor trade continue to use television advertising, while the more pervasive radio advertising is claimed to provide better results. Press advertising is still the most popular medium for business in general, while local services are well suited to direct mail. 'Cold calling' by telephone, much exploited by the double-glazing trade, can offend customers, but the carrier who has just sold a contract to a new customer may do well to remember 'buyer's remorse' and ring up soon after completing the deal to reassure the customer that all is well, and that this was a 'wise buy'.

Promotion, which includes public relations, ultimately depends upon the confidence you have in your product. If the customers do not like it there will be no repeat sales – we have already come across the slogan, 'You can promote the wrong product – once'.

Once a firm has made sure that the product is right for the market, so that it is saleable, then it must constantly monitor it, to see where changes will lead to greater sales, and these changes must then be promoted in the market. Price is important here, with tactics including the use of premium offers and tying in a customer with a long-term contract at a discount. A sound promotion campaign must be based on the existing information held by market intelligence; its progress must be followed through so its degree of success can be measured; and there must be a follow-up, to carry on the good work. Marketing management here is at the heart of good management anyway.

MARKETING MANAGEMENT IN THE TRANSPORT BUSINESS

As we have already said, in service industries like transport, production and marketing are inseparable, because the product is totally perishable, and cannot be stored. Product-based management easily forgets this, and concentrates on getting the vehicles on the road (or rail). Managers responsible for production, and for finance, may argue that marketing is a secondary function, perhaps with a marketing manager in charge. No transport business can afford this division, which for the small firm should not exist, since the proprietor fulfils all three of these functions. In the larger firm sound corporate planning should assure that every department is working together toward the same objective: getting the product, and its price, right for the market. Only then will there be a contribution to the efficiency that is the chief objective of economic policy.

It could be argued that there is no room for a marketing department in the transport firm; everyone should be involved in marketing. This is especially true in the case of personnel, because transport is about management at a distance. Engineering is concerned with drivers who are handling extremely expensive machines, and finance is concerned with everyone who is involved in selling, on the vehicles or in an office. It is accepted now that train crews and bus drivers, as well as delivery drivers who set up equipment in the office or the home, must be 'customer friendly', but training is not enough to achieve this unless the people concerned see where their job fits into the marketing objective of the company. You cannot leave this to a marketing manager; marketing must be the lifeblood of the firm, from senior management to drivers and fitters.

Nevertheless the larger firm should have a manager whose department is dedicated to the contribution that marketing makes to success. As we have seen, it must not be a bolt-on activity, but rather a central powerhouse of ideas and activities, all of them directed to the survival of the firm in its market. With the nature of that market defined and understood, the following subdivisions of the marketing department should each of them be headed by a qualified marketer:

- market intelligence;
- marketing research;
- advertising and promotion;
- new product development;
- *ad hoc* advice to management , including pricing policy, branding and image.

If the firm is not large enough to allow for each of these, then a greater responsibility must fall to the head of the marketing department.

CONCLUSION

Marketing must be the spirit and purpose of the firm, and must never be an add-on. Economic policy for transport must recognize this, and ensure that there is maximum freedom for managers to identify their market, to research and understand it, and then to offer the customers a product whose quality and price will satisfy effective demand and promote the efficiency of the economy. Public choice theory tells us that the 'administrative solution' will not promote marketing in this beneficial sense, but it must be admitted that certain sectors of the transport industry still have a good deal to learn.

Questions for discussion

1. What is special about the product of the transport industry?
2. Why do we speak of marketing management?
3. What do we mean by 'management at a distance'?

14

Efficiency, effectiveness and the seven Ps

MARKETING AND ECONOMICS

Marketing management is a process that is essential for the success and survival of the firm in a competitive market. Insofar as managers are free to pursue the objectives of the marketing mix their actions will tend to optimal efficiency in the allocation of scarce resources, and, plainly, to the satisfaction of effective demand. Efficient marketing is thus a key criterion by which the economist will assess the efficiency of the firm, and this, as we have seen, must mean the concentration of every part of the firm on the marketing of the product. But for the process to tend to greater allocative efficiency there must be a sufficient degree of competition and contestability in the market or markets concerned, and in the remaining chapters we shall examine the freedom for marketing management to function in transport in Britain today. Freedom to respond to the market is as we have seen of great importance in service industries, and nowhere more than for the transport firm, whose product perishes in the moment of production, so that failures can only have negative effects.

THE SEVEN PS IN THE MARKETING MIX

The marketing mix is a guide and a framework for action. The idea was first developed for the marketing of tangible products, but as we have seen, services differ in that the product cannot be stored, and much thought has been given to the additional elements that are needed for their efficient marketing. Because the early examples all began with P they were called 'the four Ps', and since the extra titles for services also began with P we have the 'seven Ps' of today. They are as follows:

- product (the service);
- price;
- promotion;
- place;
- people;
- process;
- physical evidence.

Let us consider each of them, how they can be defined and in terms of their importance for successful marketing in the transport industry, in the twin markets for the movement of goods and the movement of people.

The output of the product is measured either as seat miles or as capacity tonne-miles. (The dimensions of trucks and railway wagons affect their load, which is why the additional measure is required.) The difference between these figures and passenger miles, 'goods lifted' or tonne-miles performed is the measure of success or failure of marketing. The greater it is, the greater is the element of wasted output, but as we have seen the theoretical maximum can never be matched by sales, and prices must reflect this. Some operators aim to set prices against a 40 per cent average load, which allows for counterflow journeys in peak periods, or for the back-load problem. But the product must always be defined as it is seen by customers and potential customers, while price must always be seen as the customer sees it, as the combination of price and quality of service. Marketing management is about getting the product and its price right (right, that is, for the customers), but there is also the matter of knowing what your competitors' prices are when competing for a contract. For bus companies to use mileage-related fare scales, which can mean taking passengers miles out of the way and charging them for it, is to abandon any attempt to find this 'right' price.

Most people probably think that promotion means advertising and publicity, which they think is all that marketing is about. Advertising is only one part of promotion, and its effectiveness in revenue terms is not easily calculated. It has been well said that half the cost of advertising is wasted, but you can never know which half. 'Public relations' includes paying attention to the image of the company, but equally it is about letting people know that there is a new or improved bus service where they live. The heart of marketing management lies here, though, for advertising professionals are well aware of the slogan 'You can promote the wrong product – once.'

'Place' is a word with many meanings, but these can be summed up in the word 'accessibility'. Its meaning for passengers may be obvious, but for much of the industry it is about how easy it is for customers old and new to find where the office is, or its telephone number or Web site. In the tourist industry it means having the best booking agency, if you do not have your own outlets, and an effective booking and regulation process. It also means watching the market, and spotting changes in demand, for this word also means the destination, and demand for shopping or stock holding will always vary from time to time.

For all forms of transport people are central to the marketing mix, because as we saw in Chapter 13 it is the staff, or the agency staff, who are in contact with the customer, and many of them work at a distance, and not under supervision. Typical examples are:

● operational staff (drivers, couriers and so on);
● counter staff, including staff employed by booking agencies;
● receptionists and telephonists, including staff employed by call centre operators;

- inspectors, train and platform staff;
- announcers;
- car parking attendants.

In each case we find the people who can do most harm to the product, and who must be an accepted and effective part of the marketing management of the company. In service industries marketing is everyone's job. This can mean empowering drivers to develop customer service and consistency, to the extent of using an unequivocal money-back guarantee when circumstances justify it.

People are an essential element of the process, the 'how' of service delivery. Customer perceptions of the service, the product, depend upon the way it is brought to the market; the nature of its technology and the responsibility of management in the depot and the maintenance workshop; the design and purpose of vehicles and terminals, with any specialized equipment that is necessary; personnel responsibilities and human relations management; each of them take part in determining the eventual nature and standard of the service. In a firm of any size it can be only too easy for the customer to be forgotten in the complex world of management decision making, and that can be a very serious problem.

The most recent addition to the list of Ps is physical evidence, which is the visible sign that a contract of carriage exists. It is particularly significant where journeys are booked in advance, when the customer is given a ticket or other document that shows a service is to be provided. In tourism this is likely to include further information about the trip or the holiday concerned. For coach hire and the distribution and haulage trades, and rail freight, it is evidence that a contract of carriage exists, which is not discharged until the goods are delivered to the consignee. The term thus includes both setting the passenger's mind at rest, and ensuring that both the producer and the customer know what is to be done.

ECONOMICS AND THE MARKETING MIX

We saw at the start that economics turns upon the exchange of relatively scarce products, which we now understand to include services as well as goods. In Chapter 1 we identified the term catallaxy, meaning the process of exchange, forward to an uncertain future; an exchange of cash for goods or services; an exchange which should never be 'zero sum'. Unless there is ignorance or undue influence on one side or the other, each party to the bargain should feel better off. For some reason, people have come to see marketing as a means of making people buy something when they do not want to.

Nothing could be further from the truth. Even in the limited sense of advertising and promotion we saw that 'You can promote the wrong product – once'. If customers do not like it, sales will fade away, whatever you do to try to promote it, and the same goes if they do not like the mix of price and quality that they are offered. Either way, the service is the wrong product for the customer, and the customer is the ultimate judge. The demand will shrink. Even if there is no alternative to a poor quality service, those who are forced to use it will be resentful, and word will get round. If the media get to hear about it there will be the risk of exaggeration, and the bad image of the service will damage the reputation of the firm's better quality output of which customers do approve.

This is why the concept of marketing management, where everyone in the company is involved in getting the service 'right' for customers, is so important for the efficiency of the firm, and we have seen how marketing management works through the understanding and guidance of the marketing mix. Probably most transport companies attempt to manage in this way, but real efficiency and growth can come only from the full understanding of the market as process, and the constant oversight and adjustment of the product to allow for changed conditions of demand. This means engineering managers must see that prompt and effective measures when problems arise are an essential element of the marketing mix. Any element of dominance, even if in only one sector of the market, will mean that the lesson is easily forgotten, for the existence of current or potential competition in a contestable market will always mean that attention has to be paid to each and all of the seven Ps.

This of course is exactly what economists desire to see, because this means that there will be pressure for output to be efficient in the use of resources and effective in the satisfaction of demand, two achievements that are central to the objectives of economic policy. In the next three chapters we shall be examining how far managers are free to pursue these objectives, and how far their incentive to do so is constrained. We shall explain why it is necessary to be wary of over-regulation, and above all of price control, which inevitably makes the concept of the marketing mix irrelevant.

CONCLUSION

We have seen earlier that public opinion, much of which should be better informed, too often assumes that transport, especially railways and, to an increasing extent bus services, is 'exempt' from the economic principles that govern most commercial and industrial processes, and that the objective of allocative efficiency can be ignored. Satisfaction of effective demand, which is linked with efficiency, is supposed by some to be achievable by the non-commercial provision of passenger services, even to the extent of returning these services to public ownership. In these mind-sets marketing is suspect, and marketing management is not well understood. From our examination so far we have seen that active marketing management is an essential for the achievement of the central objectives of economic policy.

Questions for discussion

1. Why is marketing vital for success in the transport industry?
2. What is promotion all about?
3. What do we mean by saying 'you can promote the wrong product – once'?

15

Marketing in freight transport and distribution

COMMERCIAL STRUCTURE

Freight transport has few of the political problems faced by other modes, apart for the strictures of the environmentalists. The privately owned train companies have attracted traffic from their road competitors and coastwise shipping has achieved a new lease of life. Highway pricing continues to distort the economics of the road-based firms, but freight transport today is a productive industry like any other, only it is in the services sector. In the absence of discriminatory intervention on the part of government there would seem to be few barriers to the application of marketing management by the many firms engaged in the movement of goods.

Before we examine this further we must remember that the industry is not just made up of a large number of very similar businesses. Forms of ownership vary widely, and the importance of transport for the control of logistics means that much freight transport is a sector of manufacture and distribution, which may in practice be 'outsourced' and not provided 'in house' by the companies concerned. The status of the transport manager in industry is not usually very high, and may amount to as little as responsibility for maintaining and manning trucks.

Apart from the prevalent 'white vans', the vehicles seen on motorways and urban streets are owned by a range of different types of business. Supply chain management is the key to understanding the industry, within which the effectiveness of the transport contribution is vital to success. The most obvious examples are the trucks that carry the familiar livery of the supermarket chains, though these may well be outsourced to a specialist transport company. The night-time movement of parcels and small consignments through the 'hub-and-spoke' system supplies the needs of supply chain management as well as those of smaller businesses. Goods are collected at various terminals and despatched in the evening to hubs, almost all in the Midlands, where the items are sorted to outgoing trucks for delivery next day. This system is very efficient, causing little congestion. It has grown up spontaneously over the past 30 years, and is not open to competition from rail freight companies. Specialist vehicles are used for various needs, including the movement of fuel and other liquids, and the carriage of steel products. Many drivers are self-employed, often working by contract for larger companies, and sometimes carrying their livery. Household removal businesses are generally small and local, remaining close to their market in the same way as firms in the coaching trade. Freight transport is a much more complex industry than might at first have been thought.

BARRIERS AND OPPORTUNITIES FOR MARKETING MANAGEMENT

In any highly contestable market the effect of competition means that businesses whose marketing effort is weak will not continue to trade for long. For many general hauliers marketing means understanding your customer's needs, together with an adequate grasp of your competitors' prices. Since the average fleet is small, marketing means selling. For the larger firm, seeking longer contracts or outsourcing the firm's operations will be part of the marketing management of the customer's business. Parcels carriers have problems similar to bus companies, which we shall meet in Chapter 16, since they carry so many small consignments, and can easily lose customers without knowing it until it is almost too late. This is the opposite situation to the small contractor who has only one or two customers to satisfy at a time. Perhaps it is only for the hauliers who operate nationally that the term 'marketing management' really comes into play.

Excellence in terms of the seven Ps is attainable in the freight transport sector because of the limited effect of government intervention. Safety regulations (see Chapter 9) support the quality of the product, which as we have seen is safe delivery of the goods concerned. Price is a matter for settlement with the customer, and in a highly competitive market there will always be pressure to keep prices down. We may expect promotion to be part of the pursuit of new contracts, although parcels carriers may address the wider public. A good example is the Post Office with its slogan 'What are you going to send?'

Place can be seen to include the premises of the consignor (the customer) and the consignee, which must be taken into account when tendering for a contract, and it also involves the optimum siting for a parcels hub, including the availability of air transport for international movement. While drivers are central to the operation, so also are in-house staff who maintain records and accounts, and representatives who find new customers and negotiate contracts. People matter just as much for freight transport as they do for passenger transport, and where 'added value' is sought, drivers need more skills than just driving a truck. The driver's relationship with the customer is of central importance, but added value may also mean setting up and testing equipment such as refrigerators and computers within people's homes. Process is linked closely with place, because of the 'labyrinth movement' whereby the firm gets the best mileage from vehicles moving from one site to another. Finally, physical evidence includes the paperwork involved in the contract, as well as the role of the tachograph in recording drivers' working hours.

While the typical freight carrier has considerable freedom of operation in these terms, there remains the need to conform to the regulations governing premises, vehicles and drivers' hours. Also it must be remembered that much movement is across national borders, with national and international regulations to comply with, and further costs in terms of insurance. There may be depots in other countries to supervise, while business in the southern counties faces competition from operators based across the Channel, whose initial fuel costs are substantially lower. The proposals being discussed for satellite surveillance of such vehicles, in order to charge the firms concerned for using British roads, could lead to the general introduction here of road-use pricing, which would bring home the external costs of the industry to the operators.

CONCLUSION

In such a complex and competitive industry it is plain that marketing management is essential to survival, and it is practised in many of the larger firms. The industry benefits from a low profile in public and political opinion, which means that little intervention exists to limit the pursuit of success through the use of the seven Ps. While they may seem remote for owner-drivers and smaller firms, the mere need for survival means that they will be present for management, even if the terms are not in common use, while among the larger companies there have been examples of failure that suggest a lack of attention to the need for market-based thinking. In terms of economics, the efficiency and effectiveness of the freight transport industry, by road, rail and sea, depends upon good marketing management, as it always has.

Questions for discussion

1. What is meant by supply chain management?
2. Why do 'people' matter for freight as well as passenger transport?
3. What are freight operators actually selling?

16

Marketing in commercial road passenger transport

COMMERCIAL STRUCTURE

There are three distinctive sectors in what is generally spoken of as bus and coach operation, and each of them is subject to different degrees of regulation, although no form of price control exists for any of them. As with any generalization such as this, there is some overlap at the edges, but the differences matter more. First is the provision of local services, which are the urban and rural bus services with which we are all familiar. Second, there are the express coach services which carry passengers on fixed routes at advertised fares and time tables, and are associated with extended tours, both home and overseas, that are linked to the tourism industry. Finally there is the coaching trade, which is concerned with the private hire of vehicles and the provision of school and works services, as well as some local service operation.

Local services are mainly provided by large 'territorial' companies, almost all of them owned by large ownership groups, most of which own train operating companies as well, while several have overseas interests. There are 19 municipally owned bus companies in cities like Cardiff, Edinburgh, Nottingham and Plymouth as well as some smaller places, while many small businesses which we may call 'niche operators' supplement service provision in both urban and rural areas. Operation of express coach services and a good deal of the extended tour business is in the ownership of a few larger firms, while the coaching trade is almost entirely in the hands of small, often family businesses, based in cities, towns and villages. Only in London are bus companies subject to franchise, which severely limits their marketing freedom.

BARRIERS AND OPPORTUNITIES FOR MARKETING MANAGEMENT

While bus operators are subject to a degree of intervention that does not apply in the same way to either type of coach operator, outside London managers are free to pursue the objectives associated with the seven Ps with little constraint. The relative failure of the industry to take advantage of the freedom introduced by the Transport Acts of 1980 and 1985 suggests that they have done little to pursue them as yet. More than 20 years since the former regulatory system was removed we have yet to see the market for local bus services fully exploited, and while the long-term fall in traffic has belatedly been halted, successful market-oriented management has some way to go to deliver a product that will satisfy demand in the market.

The entire industry is subject to regulation by the Office of Fair Trading (OFT), which only became involved with the passage of the Transport Act of 1985. Its officials admitted then that they knew too little about their new responsibilities, and their policies have been confused to some extent ever since. They tend to think in terms of a market for bus services rather than a market for movement, which as we saw in Chapter 10 includes the competition of the car, as well as rail passenger services. Any attempt by bus companies to coordinate fares or to present a joint timetable over a route or section of route is condemned by the OFT, preventing operators from combining to grow the market, even though monopolistic practices in what is still a reasonably open market would soon lead to loss of custom. At the same time the OFT keeps a watchful eye on mergers, and thereby tends to maintain the unwritten arrangements that define the mutual boundaries of the larger companies.

Defining the seven Ps of service marketing is not difficult, and for the most part bus and coach companies are free to pursue them, except in London. There the bus companies are privately owned, but are franchised by Transport for London, in a system which ties management hand and foot to provide services according to the requirements laid down for them. Each franchise agreement includes long schedules of regulation, governing everything from choice of route (place) by way of promotion to the style of ticketing (physical evidence). The costly bureaucracy and the opportunities forgone by way of growing the market raise questions as to economic policy, while pressure for similar schemes in the provinces must be seen to threaten the good marketing management that is to be found there.

THE SEVEN PS IN BUS AND COACH OPERATION

We have already defined the product as the safe arrival of passengers at their destination, subject to any time schedule that may exist. Output is measured in seat-miles, sales in passenger miles, and the shortfall between output and sales is waste, because of the perishability of the product. But the quality of the product is closely linked to its price, and we emphasized in Chapter 2 that the customer sees the cost as a mixture of price and quality. There are circumstances where separate services at different levels of price and quality are justified, and many smaller firms operating local services take advantage of this, offering higher quality and lower fares. Marketing management extends to such things as showing correct destination blinds, which is a central part of customer care. Vehicle design is central to the quality of the product, with ease of access and suitable seating. Coach services require vehicles fitted with toilets as well as equipment for serving drinks and light meals, according to the distance travelled. Operators in the coaching trade may have similar requirements, but for much local work a less sophisticated vehicle is sufficient; not least where the carriage of schoolchildren is involved.

Product and price are key objectives for marketing management, yet many people think of marketing as no more than advertising. Promotion means much more than that, and unless the first two Ps are taken care of there is little point in trying to sell the product. The public image of bus and coach services is not high, and the industry as a whole could do more to improve it. Promotion should start from press, radio and television advertising designed to improve the image, as has been done in the railway industry. Getting the product known, in terms of times and fares as well as differing liveries, is central to promotion, while for coach operators it is often necessary to work through travel agencies. Promotion is about selling the product, at the price that the customer will accept. While it is sometimes said that 'the bus is its own advertisement', there is much more to promotion than that, if success is to be achieved. In the retail trades marketing effort goes into 'building the brand', and the bus industry in general has still to catch on.

The definition of place varies according to the product. For coach trips it is the destination, and also the picking-up points, but for local bus services it is more complex. For many customers the destination may be the city centre, but many others will want to go to a suburb along the route, or make a variety of intermediate trips. 'Place is where the bus goes', but marketing means finding out where the customers want to go, and providing the service they want, and are willing to pay for. Not every destination is easy of access, and here marketing management includes relationships with local authorities who may not be entirely sympathetic to transport needs.

As for all other service providers, success in bus and coach operation is ultimately dependent upon people. We saw in the box on page 16 of Chapter 2 how the loss of the conductor can now be seen as a false economy, and the bus driver is the point-of-sale member of the firm. If the driver is unpleasant, or fails to look after passengers by refusing to wait for latecomers at the bus stop, or driving harshly and making the trip unpleasant, no amount of promotion will make up for the poor image of the product. Coach drivers may have the incentive of a tip, but they often take a more personal interest in the success of the passengers' journey. While there are some notable exceptions, it may be that the weakest point in marketing management for many bus companies is the failure to recognize the importance of the 'platform staff', and the need to empower the drivers so that they can feel part of the business. Success here is essential if the process of production and sales is to function as it should. Process can be defined as the logistics of passenger transport; everything that goes on to put the vehicle in place for the customer's use, which is another way of looking at marketing management.

Physical evidence is a more subtle aspect of marketing. For trains or trams the first evidence is the visible existence of the track and the stations, which provides an element of security that may be missing when customers are waiting at the kerbside for a bus that is running late. There is an element of promotion here, which the display of 'real time' information at bus stops can best provide. But there is also the ticket, and this means the ticketing system, which gives the passenger evidence of payment having been made. It remains to be seen what the introduction of smart cards for on-vehicle payment will do for the confidence of the customer.

THE PURSUIT OF GOOD MARKETING

Coach and bus operation is a complex task, and because unsold production is lost and gone for ever, the need for all management to be marketing management is plain to see. Everything and every-one must be working together to achieve sales, and because this industry requires management at a distance, with point-of-sale staff on the road and not on the premises, the drivers and their immedi-ate supervisors must be seen to be essential for success. The larger the company, the more remote the drivers may feel from upper levels of management, which gives the smaller firms an advantage, so for the bigger bus companies devolution of responsibility within the overall unity of the firm becomes a necessity.

Internal barriers to marketing management can be overcome by reframing the company in this way, provided that the organization as a whole is seeking success, and is not hampered by bureaucracy or subject to the rent-seeking problems we discussed in Chapter 4. Functioning at its best, the company will then tend to contribute to economic efficiency, by pursuing the satisfaction of effective demand. Any system of franchise, such as that in force in London, can only work against these desirable objectives, by diverting progressively more management decisions to the administrative sector, with no such objectives, and with the distortions that are identified in public choice theory (see Chapter 5). Franchise seems to offer the successful tenderer a monopoly, but while this removes the threat of a competing operator taking advantage of failures on the part of management, it neglects the nature of the market, which once again we define as the movement of passengers, and in which the principal competitor is the private car. Successful marketing follows from the pursuit of financial reward, with willingness to undertake risk in the process. A contestable market is the only way to provide for this.

Even so there are barriers to marketing that arise from the regulatory framework within which bus and coach companies have to work today. The extent and complexity of regulation, not always justified in practice, means that a great deal of management time and effort is taken up by the system. The licensing authorities, not unlike the Office of Fair Trading, do not always seem to have the desirable insight into the nature of the industry, and tend to impose penalties that are not always just. Quality control, which is essential for a fail-dangerous industry such as transport, can actually be weakened if it is too narrowly defined. In particular, the relationship between operators and highway authorities, which is central to both efficiency and effectiveness, is only slowly being improved through the experience of Quality Partnerships. But here we must conclude that the problems of congestion and the commercial advantages of the private car will not be settled without the introduction of point-of-use road pricing, needed by coach operations as well as local bus services.

The bus industry, like the railways, attracts the enthusiast, who often remains an amateur, making comments from outside the trade. It is probably true that most transport managers, in all modes, and not a few of the people working at every level in the firm, including drivers, have an element of this interest, which makes them the more devoted to the standards of output. The contribution of the true enthusiast however is in direct proportion to his or her ability to take an objective view of the product. Marketing of course requires an objective view of the product, including its weaknesses as well as its strengths. A good test at an interview might be to ask the applicant how best to handle a complaint. If the response implies a degree of hostility to the imagined complainer, then the individual concerned is not cut out for a career in marketing. The selection and employment of personnel must contribute to a structure in which success in the market comes first, whether in engineering, finance or, as here, in the personnel department.

Another problem specific to marketing in the bus and coach industry is the relationship between operators and public authorities outside London, which is somewhat complex. Local councils have their own agenda for public transport, as have the Passenger Transport Authorities, with whom the local councils do not always agree on policy. Some recent Quality Partnerships have succeeded in attracting new passengers, but the proposed Quality Contracts promise to be more like a franchise, with the potential for marketing management to fall between the two sides. This uncertain relationship has been effective since the bus industry was deregulated and privatized in 1985.

One aspect of marketing that has suffered from divided responsibility has been the provision of bus stop signs, waiting accommodation and information. While railways and light rapid transit present clear physical evidence, bus services can seem to be more evanescent, and it is a serious marketing failure that so little attention has been paid by local authorities or bus companies to the provision of smart and effective information, that the bus goes from here.

CONCLUSION

In the background there are barriers to good marketing that arise from political interests, barriers which we saw to be largely lacking where freight transport is concerned. It seems that whatever is politically correct is also short-sighted, and such attitudes too often fail to recognize the realities of the market. 'Social exclusion' is a case in point, for good marketing management will seek out and satisfy all demand that can earn as much as a marginal contribution to the finances of the firm. It is here that the past has caught up with the industry today, for the price control that existed before 1980 prevented bus companies from offering reduced off-peak fares and other forms of discriminatory pricing and allowed this element of promotion to be taken over by local government.

Successful marketing in bus and coach operation requires maximum commercial freedom, and today that is threatened by pressure from the Passenger Transport Executives and some local authorities to take the industry back into public ownership. The belief exists that transport is not like other industries, being in some way exempt from the realities of economics. But an efficient economy demands efficient producers, in transport as much as anywhere else, and that means good marketing, which management must be free to undertake.

Questions for discussion

1. Why is it important for bus managers to define their market?
2. What could the bus industry do to improve its public image?
3. Why must bus companies and local councils work together for better marketing?

17

Marketing in railway transport

COMMERCIAL STRUCTURE

Railways have such a long history and such significance in public awareness that the application of marketing may well seem foreign to them in the eyes of people who ought to know better. They are often seen as a monopoly industry, despite the fact that they are in competition with alternative modes of transport, so we have to repeat once again that there is a market for the movement of goods and a market for the movement of passengers, and that success in each of them requires sound marketing management. But for far too long railway managers saw their responsibility to be running trains, with no great concern about what was carried in them, however little.

As we saw in Chapter 11, the government took an interest in regulating railways from the beginning, and by the end of the 19th century this extended to controlling rates and charges. A manager who is unable to set the firm's prices has no freedom for marketing management at all. This intervention extended to restructuring in 1921 and to nationalizing in 1947. Privatization when it came in 1993 was not only confused, but meant little by way of independent commercial decision taking. Today the railway companies remain as much the concern of government as they have been throughout their history, this despite the fact that railways account for a small percentage of movement in the market at large.

The creation of Railtrack, which was not in fact a requirement of the directive of the European Commission, detached a large part of railway management from the marketing process, and neither Railtrack plc nor its successor could have any rigorous concept of what was meant by a customer. Yet as far as the train and freight operating companies (TOCs and FOCs) are concerned, their dependence upon the track provider for access to their own customers makes the situation more complicated than would seem to be necessary. The TOCs and the FOCs are in competition with each other in obtaining access. The task of sorting out these problems, and of managing the system of franchises for the TOCs, rests with the Rail Regulator and the Strategic Rail Authority, whose decisions are subject to further intervention by HM Treasury. It is all rather a muddle.

It seems to have been assumed at first that successful franchisees would by the end of the franchise period have paid off the entrance fee and be ready to take over as independent commercial enterprises. This no longer seems to be part of government policy, leaving an element of ambiguity in the business of passenger movement. Marketing management is in one sense a day-to-day activity, but it also requires longer-term planning, which for the TOCs is limited by the remaining length of the franchise. The fully commercial 'ethical franchise', which is familiar in fast food and many other outlets, includes a form of partnership, allowing for agreed initiative to arise from either partner, but no comparable relationship exists for the management of the TOCs. The great advantage of the system compared with 'British Rail plc', which some proposed in 1993, is the opportunity for various product and marketing initiatives to appear, which a single company would find it difficult to achieve.

THE SEVEN PS AND THE RAILWAY

For many years it was traditional to refer to 'the railway service', and for a long time operating staff were defined as 'railway servants'. This in part reflects the fail-dangerous nature of railway operation, which we examined in Chapter 11, and which led some authors to regard the industry as being almost of a military nature. As with shipping and aviation, uniforms were issued, and a clear hierarchy of management rose from the locomotive driver up to the senior manager in his Crombie overcoat and bowler hat. Those days are gone, but the quasi-military structure remains, with the traditional distinction between 'line and staff'. Track maintenance and train operation were always regarded as 'line' functions, taking priority over 'staff' functions, such as marketing. Pricing, as we shall see, was another matter, but since pricing is central to marketing, the pattern of railway management was distorted, with costing, as we have seen, neglected until the years after 1947.

The traditional loyalty to the service has been said to be the greatest loss that followed from privatization, and this has been complicated further by the decision to separate track from operation. In short, people is now something of an issue. The working relationship and connection between engineers and operators has been broken, with disastrous results, which have seriously damaged the image of railway travel, and marketing management can never function where impervious walls exist between departments. Where the division is between separate businesses, as between the train operators and Railtrack (or its successor), and where, as we shall see, it confuses pricing policy on either side, then it is hard to see how railway marketing can be pursued with any great effect.

The special place of rail transport in the eyes of the public, and from the first in the eyes of government, has meant that it is still treated as if it is not suited for free commercial management. It is as if those responsible for railway policy cannot trust the management of the industry to operate as any other kind of business should, and this is most striking in the case of price. Controls of fares and charges were largely removed in the days of British Railways in 1962, and the freedom of railway managers to develop market-based pricing contributed to the improved performance that followed. Privatization however included powers for the state to intervene, where passenger fares are concerned, and the Strategic Rail Authority is still involved with this issue. In terms of both economics and marketing, this is to strike at the essential freedom of management: to set its own prices in the market. The railways now face an impossible situation, in which fares have remained too low to justify the new investment which they need, while at the same time they are seen by the public to be too high, despite the fact that passenger carryings are higher than they have been for many years. Management is thus presented with a 'double bind', which the Strategic Rail Authority cannot find it easy to escape except by increased subsidy – itself a very difficult political issue. In this situation, marketing management must be very difficult to achieve.

Discussion of the product raises further problems for marketing. The quality of passenger services varies widely, while the years of under-investment after 1947, together with the impact of recent accidents, make the problem of delays owing to work on the infrastructure likely to continue for some time. Reliability ranks high in passengers' requirements, and poor timekeeping reflects directly upon the image of the railway. Comfort and customer care also rank high, but some would argue that speed – expressed as 'lapsed time' for a point-to-point journey – is less important than other aspects of production. These problems make for difficulties in promotion, which was also neglected for so long, and which is largely undertaken by the principal Train Operating Companies. But the marketing slogan 'You can promote the wrong product – once' is all too well illustrated by the problem of promoting commuter services in London and the south-east.

The difficulties involved with place were well illustrated when it became manifestly necessary to close many lines and stations in order to preserve the financial stability of British Railways, while today there is pressure to reopen some of these lines, which raises serious issues in terms of economics, as we saw in Chapter 11. In marketing terms it is necessary to recognize the emotional involvement of some lobbyists, but also to sympathize with the people for whom the railway station is a symbol of opportunity, whether they use it a great deal or not.

It is however the process of production, the logistics of getting the train to make its way over the correct lines at the advertised times and with the appropriate rolling stock and the correct staff, that is so much more complex for railway management than it is for road transport. Central to the process is the importance of the infrastructure, track, terminals and signalling; but while track and signalling must function safely and effectively, it is at the 'terminals', the railway stations, that direct marketing comes into place. For many years the station master was the key figure, with overall responsibility, and there has been criticism of the separation of function within this area of responsibility. However that may be, the 'railway problem' will not go away unless the nature of the process is seen to be central to marketing management.

CONCLUSION

With changes so recent and still continuing in the railway industry, it is difficult to avoid areas of controversy, but since we are seeking to achieve sound economic objectives, and since these are linked to effective marketing management, it is impossible to escape the conclusion there this is an industry which has been hampered throughout its life by state and political intervention, and that the seven P's are still highly problematic.

Questions for discussion

1. Could railways be so important that they do not need marketing management?
2. What does the separation of track from trains mean for marketing?
3. How can the railway overcome its bad public image today?

Part four

Summary and conclusions

18

Conclusion: no attainable end-state

WHERE WE COME FROM

All economics stems from the conclusion, based on observation, that millions of buy/not-buy decisions constantly being made act as signals to entrepreneurs and established businesses in a form of spontaneous organization that we call a market. The outcome can never approach an exact balance of demand and supply, which could be said to 'clear the market', for there are too many uncertainties to be found in what may be called the economic process, or catallaxy. We can only say that some factors may 'tend to' a better balance, while others may push the process off course. In an ideal world the process would tend to solve the great problem that faces us: how to arrive at the fairest available allocation of the scarce resources of the planet while at the same time satisfying the effective demand of millions of people, worldwide. The problem that faces us arises from scarcity. It is an ancient problem, and economics identifies two methods of tackling it, the market solution and the administrative solution. When we address what has been called the transport problem it is important to understand the difference, for neither of them is perfect.

For some authors and people in public life the question does not seem to arise, for it is assumed that transport is in some way exempt from the economic processes we have been looking at, and should be provided by government, national or local. That implies that it is the responsibility of administrators and not of profit-seeking businesses. The experience of planned economies during the 20th century has shown the weakness of this solution, and where it has been attempted in a more open economy the rigidity of the administration has tended to restrict the economic efficiency of the industry concerned, since bureaucracy is not well fitted to respond to the myriad of messages that are to be heard in the market all the time. Neither has it tended to the satisfaction of effective demand, as the reputation of the former British Rail would suggest.

While there have been many examples of this problem in the provision of transport services, it is still more problematic where investment decisions are concerned, whether in the infrastructure or in new rolling stock. Opportunity cost should be the prime concern for decisions in both the private and the public sector of the economy, but whereas private businesses must suffer the cost of any mistaken investment, the same discipline does not apply to the administrative sector. While forecasting may be hazardous, accountancy techniques exist to compare the return on investment against alternatives, or against long-term interest rates, whereas in the public sector it is open to government to ignore these and to approve investment that is claimed to be in the public interest, which, of course, is something impossible to measure.

To say that the market solution is the ideal solution is to forget that no market can function perfectly, and that the most we can expect is that market forces will 'tend to' a solution that is in any case unattainable, because of the uncertainties of the future. We saw in Part One that there are problems due to market failures and other problems arising from regulatory failures, and the aim of economic policy for transport is to get the best achievable balance in dealing with each of them. But since it is economic policy that we are talking about, it follows that the market solution is to be preferred, with whatever measures may be needed to deal with its failures. And this must be as true for transport as it is for any part of the economy.

The uncertainty of the future alone explains why a perfect market is unattainable, even before we allow for human weakness. As Adam Smith observed it is the selfish decisions of buyers and sellers that come together to balance demand and supply and so tend to economic efficiency. It is not from benevolence that the bus company makes it possible for us to get to places where we want to be; it is because the directors seek to make a living out of what we are prepared to pay. Managers who fail to identify and provide for demand stand to lose by their mistakes, and in an open market they will lose out to their competitors. The same thing will follow from failure to match the mix of price and quality to that which the customers, within their available spending power, would prefer to have available.

One reason why the process does not always work is human failure. Running a business is not easy, and while the entrepreneur is driven by the hope of future profit, the element of risk is always there. Those who provide for our demand do not like competition, and will take steps to avoid it where they can. Economies of scale enable companies to grow until people in the organization forget that sales come first, and pursue the popular objective of a quiet life. We have seen how good marketing management is only too easily missed, and this is especially likely when the business is divided into separate sections divided by 'Chinese walls'. 'Rent seeking' appears when staff at any level claim a greater benefit than their employment might be seen to justify. It is not easy to identify, and the normal pressures of business restrict it in ways that are not found in its equivalent in the public sector, but it arises as a problem where monopoly exists. Market failure is found when the relationship of demand and supply is out of balance, and may follow from weaknesses in marketing management, which are not uncommon in public transport today. It may also follow from administrative failure, as in the case of the regulation of bus services, or of external costs that have not been brought to book. Needless to say, for road transport, freight or passenger (including the private car), in the absence of road-use pricing there can only be market failure on a large scale, which administrative failure can only tend to make worse.

Administrative failure can be found when regulators charged with rectifying the consequences of market failure intervene and make things worse, or it can follow from intervention in pursuit of policy objectives by government and politicians, whether central or local. Since these objectives are effectively party-political, supported or opposed by elected representatives, what may be called the vote motive is likely to be involved, down to the diversion of a bus route along a particular street. More broadly, policy objectives are associated with the 'administrative solution', tending invariably to restrict competition in the market.

Economists who have analysed these issues have developed public choice theory, which accounts for many of the weaknesses that follow from administrative intervention. It makes no difference whether the objective is to correct market failures or to restrict the market process itself: it is a form of rent seeking, where members of the administrative caste, or bureaucrats, seek their own advantage as well as pursue that immeasurable objective, the public interest. The economics of public choice recognizes something that has traditionally been ignored: that administrators are themselves economic agents who will seek their own satisfactions along with their own set tasks. It cannot be assumed, as it was for so long, that they will always put their public responsibilities before their personal and very understandable agenda. This is not to imply corruption, but rather the pursuit of increased status and income, for example by devising reasons to have larger departments and more staff. In recent years entrepreneurs have tapped into this market, with the remarkable growth in the number of expensive conferences at which administrators as well as policy makers are present.

IGNORANCE AND UNCERTAINTY

Inherent in the nature of the catallaxy is the uncertainty of the future. While firms in the market must be involved constantly in forecasting demand and insuring against uncertainty, business history contains many examples of failure arising from policies that depend too closely upon too rigid a plan. Public authorities are particularly vulnerable to this, not least when elected representatives commit themselves to planning for some ideal end-state which economics assumes can never exist. (Economists have been said, not without reason, to be able to explain why outcomes which they had forecast were not achieved.) The law of large numbers makes it possible to construct a forecast on the basis of a small unbiased sample, while existing trends can be assumed, with 'incremental smoothing', to continue more or less unchanged. But something more is required for survival in a competitive market, where the results of the calculations may come through too late.

Economics assumes that the market process, if left alone, will tend to the optimum allocation of scarce resources and the general satisfaction of effective demand. Neither objective can be achieved to perfection, because there can be no perfect solution to the transport problem in a world of uncertainty. There will be many problems, such as external costs and benefits, that require intervention where the market process is imperfect, but public choice theory points to the danger that intervention may make things worse. The idea, present in the minds of many politicians and members of the public, that there could be a perfect solution such as perhaps other countries have achieved, is inherently false. All we are permitted is to seek to improve the way transport works, and economics concludes that firms in competition, whatever their weaknesses, will have the best incentive to do it.

There are two reasons that economic policy for transport may still fail if the administrative solution is chosen, public choice theory apart. The first is the problem of scale and structure, which applies to any over-large organization, including many in the private sector. While the relationships of supply and demand and the adjustments of price and quality produce signals in the market through the myriads of buy/not-buy decisions, in a large and monolithic organization, public or private, it is flatly impossible for all that information to be brought together at one place and at one point in time. Even if that were possible it would already be out of date, and any administrative response could only have effect long after the situation had changed.

There is a further diseconomy of large scale here, to be found in both private and public corporations. Where the structure of the business is like a pyramid, managers at the top are remote from the information that floods the market. An increasing amount tends to get lost as it rises through the system, or may only arrive after it is out of date. Intermediate levels of management may filter the information to serve their own ends. Instructions from the top also pass through levels where they may become confused, and they are likely to be even more behind the times when they reach the staff working in the market itself. Where knowledge of the market and rapid response decisions are essential for survival, in much of freight transport and in the coaching trade, firms remain small, while bigger businesses need to look to their marketing management to see that the whole firm responds to the flow of information, if they are to survive. Bureaucracy is everywhere the enemy of efficiency, and the administrative solution leads to structures that do not have the same incentive to understand and respond to the market. During the second half of the 20th century experience in the nationalized railway and in the sectors of the bus industry that were state or municipally owned demonstrated the problems that arise from the administrative solution.

The second problem facing all long-range planning, and one that demonstrates again the weakness of the administrative solution, arises from the emergence of chaos theory in the natural sciences, which is now being applied to the function of human organizations and of economies. 'Chaos' is an intricate mixture of order and disorder, such as any traffic manager will recognize. What its study has shown is that dynamic processes , such as those we see in the market, are 'non-linear', tending exponentially to ever greater uncertainty. Even quite small errors in management can increase the instability of any system, and to stick to a business plan over-much dependent upon the assumption of linear dynamics can only lead to serious failures.

The administrative solution has the inherent disadvantage that bureaucracy and political commitment make it very difficult for such an organization to respond to this state of affairs. Adaptation to the uncertainty that affects all planned systems is really only meaningful where firms compete in the market, which allows for spontaneous reactions to unpredictable change, so long as the firm is organized to permit them. It is just in this way that the need for the entrepreneur is plain. On the other hand over-regulation, from which the transport industry suffers, conflicts with the need for freedom to react to shifts in demand or to explore new sectors of the market. High taxation has a similar effect, while the very nature of monopoly, which private sector management may be tempted to pursue, is opposed to spontaneity and change.

Yet in favouring the market solution the economist must avoid a narrow-minded advocacy of the freedom of private firms to pursue their own objectives in the catallaxy. Today's society is extremely complex, but people live in hope that problems will be solved and a better state of affairs will be achieved. What they expect of the state is what they expect of private enterprise: a vision of better things. Municipal pride and market success need not be in opposition. Administrators must recognize the importance of the signals to be found in the market, and transport managers must recognize the place of government and government servants in seeking a better future for us all. And those who manage in either sector must learn to talk to and understand each other. Wealth comes from trade, and the public sector has no claim to moral superiority over private industry, where profits are sought from the satisfaction of effective demand.

NO IDEAL END-STATE

Economic policy for the transport industry must complement and encourage its freedom to pursue the objectives which in the market economy will be found: allocative efficiency and consumer effect-iveness. The spontaneous market economy, so long as it is not distorted, will always tend to these desirable objectives, while administrative intervention will always be at risk of preventing them. At the same time the weaknesses of selfish human nature can lead to market failures which may require some degree of intervention, but only such as is compatible with 'restoring the balance'. Public choice theory explains how administrators and government officials will always tend to strengthen control, placing their own agenda before the policies that they or the politicians have devised. But while this leads us to criticize the public sector we must not forget that bureaucrats are to be found in the private sector too. The diseconomies of large scale that we have identified present their own problems, and the existence of rent-seeking in large private businesses, which are not uncommon in the transport industry, can produce outcomes that are comparable with those identified by the economics of public choice.

Because of the perishability of the product of all service industries, the health of the transport economy depends upon good marketing management. The industry is open to criticism for its weaknesses in that matter, chiefly in public passenger transport, where for far too long managers failed to recognize that the chief competitor is the private car. This leads us back to the central and most serious criticism of economic policy, for freight as well as passenger movement, which is the irrational and distortive effect of the way road users pay for their track. If this were to be rectified by some form of point-of-use road pricing much of today's government intervention, safety standards apart, would no longer be necessary.

We have seen in recent years that government can intervene to promote a competitive market, as has been done for electricity, gas and telecommunications. We have also seen how government can backtrack on this, by reversing the process for the railways. The superiority of the market solution leads to the conclusion that the administrative solution has too many weaknesses for it to dominate economic policy for transport. Attempts to move to a totally administrative structure have been found to fail, as indeed public choice theory tells us that they must. Satisfying demand means a lean organization, committed to quick response, but flexible in its reaction to the uncertainties of the market. That this will tend to satisfy effective demand is obvious, but the remarkable fact is that it will tend always to allocate scarce resources to their most efficient use.

No economy could ever be planned. An open economy has its weaknesses, but any superior method of satisfying demand combined with the economic use of resources has yet to be found. The idea seems to exist in the public mind that a perfect solution could somehow be attained for what we rightly call 'the transport problem'. Unfortunately the administrative solution will tend to make the problem worse, if plans are made to achieve an unattainable perfection. Economists recognize that the point of equilibrium with perfect market clearing is a concept that has its uses in theory but is unattainable in practice. What we have called the catallaxy is a process into an unknowable future, which means that there can be no ideal end-state towards which it is possible to plan. It is thus the function of the entrepreneur to seek to second-guess the outcome, and to take the risks involved in that process. The transport industry is not in some mysterious way exempt from this, so the function of economic policy must be to encourage the freedom of transport firms to pursue it.

Questions for discussion

1. What does the uncertainty of the future mean for economic policy?
2. What do we really mean by 'the public interest'?
3. Can we ever have a transport industry with no problems at all?

Appendix 1

The elastic band

The formula for expressing elasticity of demand is:

$$\frac{\text{\% change in demand}}{\text{\% change in price}}$$

Thus if a 10 per cent increase in fares produces a 3 per cent reduction in passenger journeys (ie proportionately less than the increased price), demand is said to be inelastic at –0.3.

Other possible examples (Line 1 is the base line):

	Fare	Change	Passengers	Revenue	Elasticity
1	10p	None	100	£10.00	Unknown
2	9p	−10%	103 (+3%)	£9.27	0.3 inelastic
3	11p	+10%	97 (−3%)	£10.67	0.3 inelastic
4	9p	−10%	110 (+10%)	£10.67	1.0 neutral
5	9p	−10%	115 (+15%)	£10.35	1.5 elastic
6	11p	+10%	85 (−15%)	£8.50	1.5 elastic

Note the effect of different elasticities on revenue. It appears safe to increase fares where demand (as on commuter services) is inelastic; indeed, to lower fares would simply lose revenue. Conversely, where demand is inelastic (as on shoppers' services) increased fare will lose revenue, whereas a reduction may bring increased revenue.

The same principle applies to all modes of transport. But note: you can only be certain about the actual elasticity after you have changed the price. (In practice we assume that it will be 'the same as last time', all other things being equal.)

CROSS-ELASTICITY OF DEMAND

With this we set out to measure what happens to demand for one commodity when prices are changed for another. Clearly there must be some relationship between the two; either one is a substitute for the other, within broad limits (eg whether to go to the station by bus or by taxi), or the two are complementary (eg cars and motor insurance).

The formula for simple elasticity of demand is given above. For cross-elasticity of demand between commodity A and commodity B it is as follows:

$$\frac{\% \text{ change in demand for A}}{\% \text{ change in the price of B}}$$

Note that where the two may be seen to be close substitutes the resulting figure will be positive, whereas if they appear to be complementary it will be negative.

It is important to remember two conditions which apply to all calculations of elasticities. First, perceived cost can vary with changes in quality where the money price remains constant. Increasing quality at constant prices cheapens the commodity, while decreasing quality has the reverse effect. Second, like all elasticity calculations, this one can only be done after the price or the quality has changed, by which time it will probably be too late to help, except as a warning for the next time. What matters is the need to be aware of the existence of the relationship.

Appendix 2

Glossary of economic and related terms

Allocated costs   Costs that can be allocated to a particular service. Most *variable* costs can be allocated reasonably easily; some *fixed* costs can be allocated (eg on a per train/mile or per loco/mile basis), but the allocation of central costs (eg headquarters establishment) may have to be arbitrary.

Average costs   The *total costs* of the firm for a given period (usually the previous financial year), divided by the total unit mileage (eg bus/miles, train/miles, etc).

Average cost pricing   Common practice in British Rail before *price discrimination* was introduced in the 1960s. It was standard practice in the bus industry for many years, but has faded since price control was withdrawn in 1980; it has never been common in road haulage. It leads to cross-subsidization, by charging some customers more and others less than they would subjectively decide the journey was worth.

Avoidable costs, sometimes called Escapable costs   Costs that would be 'escaped' if a given service or quantum of mileage were not operated. Thus *labour costs* for one journey would not be escaped by withdrawing it, if it was part of the driver's guaranteed period of duty.

Breakeven policy   The Transport Act 1947 required transport in state ownership to earn sufficient to cover costs attributable to operation 'taking one year with another'. Many municipal transport undertakings followed the same policy, sometimes called 'non profit making'. It must be remembered that the calculations required depend a great deal upon the *capital gearing* of the business. Most authors on management regard this as an unattainable objective, and thus one that inhibits efficiency.

Capital   The stock of goods required for the production of other goods, or, as in transport, of services. It is divided into fixed and circulating capital – durable goods, such as buildings, plant and machinery; and stocks which are constantly being used up and replaced. It is not always clear where vehicles belong, especially if they are leased. The total capital of a business is however expressed in the money invested in its capital.

Capital gearing   A company is said to be 'highly geared' if it has a high percentage of fixed interest capital (eg preference shares, debentures and long-term loans) to its *equity capital*. Companies can vary considerably in their capital gearing.

Cartel   The state of affairs in which firms restrain mutual competition by agreements setting levels of price and/or output, in order to increase profitability or to stabilize revenues. The most common example in transport is the Shipping Conference, but inter-governmental agreements concerning civil aviation have produced something very much like an international cartel. A cartel depends for its success upon the level of *contestability* of its market, which is one reason why tramp shipping is less subject to cartelization than the liner trades. If it is to function, a cartel must set its prices high enough to allow its least efficient members to make *profits*, but not so high as to encourage its more efficient members to undercut. It is generally agreed that cartels cause harm to consumers by seeking to create and exploit a *monopoly* situation. In UK and US law they are illegal, but their policing is often difficult.

Cash flow The flow of money payments into and out of a firm. 'Negative cash flow' is a euphemism for making a loss.

Collective goods, sometimes called Public goods Goods (or services) that, when made available, will necessarily benefit a large number of people, who in their turn cannot be charged for the quantity they 'consume'. A standard example is the provision of street lighting. Collective goods and services are usually produced by state or non profit making organizations.

Commodities The output of the productive process; goods or services that have specified characteristics and a time and place at which they can be exchanged for money. In UK law they must be of warrantable quality, ie they must be as good as they are stated to be. In *service industries*, like transport, they are instantaneously perishable.

Complementary commodities The demand for two (or more) products may be so closely linked that a rise in the price of one leads to a fall in demand for the other. A standard example is that of petrol and cars; another might be cinema tickets and bus fares. The relationship is not permanent – a shift to electric cars would change the first example, just as the spread of television has changed the second.

Consumer surplus This arises when purchasers are charged less than their subjective assessment of the *utility* of a commodity to them. It is measured as the shortfall of the price from the maximum that purchasers would be prepared to pay – if, that is, it is possible to measure it at all. In so far as it means that other purchasers are having to pay more than their subjective assessment, in order to gain any benefit at all, it acts as a *transfer payment*, often from the poor to the rich.

Contestability   The relative ease with which new *entrepreneurs* can enter and leave a market. It may be partially or even totally limited by *natural monopoly*, by *regulation*, or by substantial *sunk costs*. The touchstone of a fully contestable market is the possibility of 'hit-and-run' competition.

Contributory revenue   Revenue over and above *avoidable costs* which may be properly transferred to other uses – eg revenue arising on a branch line in respect of traffic passing to destinations elsewhere on the system, which, after deducting avoidable costs associated with the branch, may contribute toward meeting system costs.

Coordination   The coordination of supply with *effective demand* at a given level of price, being thus related to effective delivery of the product. In a centralized economy it is the function of the bureau-cracy to ensure coordination, while in a market economy it is the function of the *entrepreneurs*. It is not the same as *integration*, which is a method of seeking to achieve it through central ownership or control. (There is a separate meaning, which is about arranging connections between passenger services, either within or between modes.)

Correlation   A statistical technique for measuring the extent to which changes in one variable (eg personal incomes) are associated with changes in another (eg demand for travel). It cannot be too often remarked that correlation does not necessarily imply causality – the reasons for a high correlation may be quite arbitrary, or there may be a third variable that is causing the correlation to arise between the first two.

Cost/benefit analysis   A technique which attempts to analyse and quantify the social costs and social benefits of investment, which will be *externalities* in financial appraisal. Thus in assessing the costs of a new airport or runway there will be welfare loss associated with noise, street congestion, etc, which are not 'brought to book' by traditional accounting procedure. In the case of a new commuter railway or LRT line there may be time savings to regular travellers and savings to motorists who find the streets less congested. Very considerable difficulties arise in making the calculations – eg, how to define the value to the individual of small amounts of time saved – and the technique has not been as effective as at one time it promised to be. See also *social cost/benefit analysis.*

Cross-subsidization, Cross-subsidy   Strictly defined, the situation in which a *transfer payment* arises, because revenue in one part of a network fails to cover *avoidable costs,* and so requires the undertaking to extract *monopoly profit* elsewhere. For obvious reasons passenger transport firms tend to extract the surplus from the poorer customers, whose *income elasticity of demand* is low, so as to support operations in wealthier districts, where the total volume of demand is low. The term is also loosely used to describe the varying levels of *cash flow* that will arise at different times and places in any transport system, as they will in any other type of enterprise. The latter use refers to a process which benefits all customers, to varying degrees. Most economists regard cross-subsidy in the first, or 'vicious' form as undesirable, better replaced with *transparent subsidy* from public funds.

CTP   Initials of the Common Transport Policy, required by the Treaty of Rome but so far failing to be achieved. Since the CAP (Common Agricultural Policy) has been an economic disaster this may be as well.

Current costs   In investment policy, these are the costs of replacing assets as they currently arise, in contrast to *historic costs* which are those that applied when the assets were acquired. The difference may follow from inflation, but can also be caused by changes in technology, as when road goods vehicles became markedly more complex in the late 1960s, making it difficult for small firms to replace their fleets. The consequence was a period of severe price competition, distortion of the market, and many business failures.

Debentures   Fixed interest securities issued in return for long-term loans. Interest is payable whether the firm makes a *profit* or not, and if it is not paid, debenture holders can force a *liquidation,* in which their claim on the available assets ranks ahead of all other shareholders.

Deficit financing   A situation in which a business (almost always publicly owned) runs at a continuing loss, and its deficit is made up from public funds at the end of the year. It applied to British Railways from about 1957, and is generally seen to be self-defeating, since it gives no incentive to managers to be either *efficient* or *effective*. The *Public Service Obligation (PSO)* was developed as an alternative, while bus firms from 1968 to 1986 were given a pre-determined *network subsidy* in return for providing services judged by local government to be socially necessary.

Demand curve   A diagram with price on the vertical axis and quantity sold on the horizontal axis, showing the relationship between the two. Because sales tend to rise with falling prices the curve usually slopes downward from left to right, its steepness depending upon the actual behaviour of consumers.

   Although most curves are drawn as a straight line, the relationship may in fact be 'sticky', depending on people's inertia in responding to changes in price. An exceptional case may be where rising prices are expected to continue, and people buy more for a time in order to economize later.

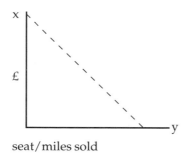

seat/miles sold

Note that the curve represents a series of points, at each of which the sales of y will vary according to the price, x. A number of things, such as relative *scarcity* (known or expected), the availability of new *substitutes*, or just changes in consumer taste, may shift the curve.

Depreciation   The reduction in value of an asset (eg a vehicle) due to its use ('wear and tear'), which has the effect of constantly diminishing the firm's *capital*. It therefore ranks as a cost, to be allowed for before determining any *profit*. Difficulties arise when there is a marked divergence between *historic* and *current* costs, or where there is a substantial element of *sunk cost,* as in a seaport or a highway. There is also a special case called *obsolescence,* which arises when technological progress makes assets 'out of date' before they have been fully depreciated; the standard example is the electric tramcar, which ceased to be a viable asset when consumers demonstrated a preference for the motor bus. (This may also be an example of 'over-investment', through failure to anticipate change.) Obsolescence is built in to the motor car, in order to keep production lines busy and so, through *economies of scale,* to keep the price of cars within consumers' reach; it is represented by the sharp fall in the value of a new car as soon as the purchaser takes delivery. Normal depreciation is provided for over a preset period, either by an equal amount each year, or by an amount increasing with age. Thus a fully depreciated vehicle may appear more profitable to operate. Unless the appropriate sums are actually placed in a 'sinking fund', depreciation is an accounting convention.

Derived demand There are very few examples of transport being wanted for its own sake (it is of course a cost to the user), and probably none in freight transport. Demand is therefore said to be derived from the demand for the satisfactions that it enables its users to obtain. Demand for freight transport and distribution is derived from the increase in value resulting from moving goods from A to B, while for passengers it is the provision of access to various satisfactions.

Diminishing marginal returns If the input of one *factor of produc-tion,* say *capital,* is increased, while input of the others is held constant, then, 'other things being equal', returns on the productive process will reach a point at which they turn down. This point seems to have been reached and passed in some public passenger transport undertakings in which serious over-staffing led to rising deficits, which were transformed into surplus by reducing man-power upon privatization.

Discount A trader may offer discount, eg for prompt payment, because your money is worth more now than it would be later. This is not because of inflation, but it reflects, notionally at least, the interest forgone on the money the trader might otherwise have placed on deposit at the bank. In economics, revenue forgone is a cost (see *opportunity cost*).

Discounted cash flow (DCF)   When alternative investments, with a fairly long revenue-earning life, are compared, it is necessary to allow for the effect of *discount,* which may lead to the conclusion that the 'cheaper', today, is actually the more expensive. See Figure 1.1 for an example. DCF calculations enable us to judge more effectively the *opportunity cost* of capital in any substantial investment, and the technique is essential as part of *cost/benefit analysis.*

Diversification   A management strategy that involves investment in activities new to the firm, although usually associated with its current operations. In the 1930s the Great Western Railway diversified into air transport; in recent years some bus companies have diversified into coach operation, and some coach firms have started running bus services. Diversification into managing a chain of public houses may not seem so unusual when it is considered that running buses is also a 'people-oriented' activity. *Holding companies* may be involved in a diverse range of activities, but the term is not generally used in such cases. The purpose of diversification is to improve *cash flow,* often because this is falling in the firm's existing activities.

EC   The European Community, responsible among other things for the development of a *Common Transport Policy.* Note that it is no longer correct to refer to the 'EEC'.

Economic efficiency   Efficiency in the allocation and use of scarce resources, so that waste and technological inefficiency are minimized. Prices determined in the market are seen by economists as by far the most effective way to achieve these aims. The 'Pareto optimum' would be achieved if resources were so allocated that no change is possible such that someone is made better off and no one worse off.

Economic rent   The earnings of a *factor of production* over and above what would be needed to keep it in its present use. Buses will continue to be used for providing services as long as they are earning enough to cover their costs so as to stay in that business; anything they earn above this is 'rent'. (See *opportunity cost*.) Problems arise in calculating the economic rent associated with the provision of a motorway, because its use is not priced (see *road-use pricing*).

Economies of scale   Where a firm has a high proportion of *direct costs*, any increase in output that can be sold so as to achieve a satisfactory return will have the effect of lowering *unit cost*. Thus the greater proportion of direct to total cost in the liner trade, in comparison with tramp shipping, suggests a reason why liner firms are larger than firms in the tramping sector. Economists have concluded that economies of scale are very limited in road transport, which would account for the small average size of fleet in road freight transport and charter coach operation, but leaves unanswered the tendency for bus firms to be relatively large.

Economies of scope   A firm which expands by acquiring a firm or firms in the same trade may be able to make considerable *economies of scale* if as a result its *unit costs* fall. In transport, among other activities, there may be further economies arising from the ability to optimize the use of the assets of the combined firms. Thus it may be possible to optimize the traffic flow over three parallel railways if they are in common ownership. Economies of scope are 'one-off' benefits, and can be exploited only up to the limit of managerial competence, before 'diseconomies of scale' (remoteness of management, etc) set in. The notion of *goodwill* may be associated with the potential for economies of scope (sometimes called rationalization).

Effective demand   For any group of products, eg movement, there is a *generic need*, which translates itself into demand for a specific product at a particular point in space and time. In economics the concept is only meaningful if the demand is supported by willingness to pay. We may all have a demand for first-class air or train travel, but for most of us, spending our own money, standard class is what we are prepared to pay for.

Effectiveness   A firm may be highly efficient (see *economic efficiency*), but may not be able to deliver the product effectively – ie, to the satisfaction of *effective demand*. The divergence will ultimately adjust itself, but in an *imperfect market* this may take some time, during which consumers will lack optimum satisfaction.

Elasticities   These reflect and measure the relative speed with which consumers will react to changes in the cheapness of a product. (This may be its price, or its mix of price and quality – higher quality at the same price makes the product cheaper, and lower quality at the same price makes it dearer.) For *demand elasticities* see Appendix 1.

Elasticities of supply may be highly significant in transport eg the short life of a minibus makes it easier for the firm to adjust its output to changes in demand.

Entrepreneur   The *factors of production* can have little to contribute to consumer satisfaction unless someone is prepared to accept the risk inherent in any business activity. Without this contribution the factors will not 'fructify'. Entrepreneurs are classified as 'arbitrageurs', who make gains from existing price differences; 'speculators' (who have a very important part to play) and 'innovators', who hope to make gains from changes in price and / or quality over time. Large corporations seek to minimize the risk involved in all business, but succeed only in postponing the day of reckoning – as has been well illustrated by the railway industry worldwide.

Escapable costs – see *avoidable costs*.

Equilibrium   An imaginary state in which the demands of consumers are exactly matched to the available supply at a given price. The interaction of supply and demand, and the adjustment of prices (the 'higgling of the market') will tend toward but never actually achieve equilibrium, which is thus not a 'steady state' (or an ideal objective of policy).

Equity capital   The residual value of a company's assets, after deducting all previous liabilities (eg taxes, wages and salaries) outstanding, creditors, and the rights of *debenture* holders and *preferential* shareholders in the event of a *winding-up*. This is in effect the residual value of the company's *ordinary shares*, which are therefore referred to as its 'equity'. This in turn reflects the fact that the equity shareholders carry the greatest risk (and should therefore have the greatest say in how the company is managed).

Externalities   Costs, and benefits accruing to individuals having no interest in the financial success of the firm. A standard example is that of the beekeeper who gains when the neighbouring farmer sows clover, but loses if the farmer sprays insecticide, yet no payment takes place between the beekeeper and the farmer to adjust the gain or the loss. In transport, pollution and congestion are examples of external cost, but external benefits are less common.

Factors of production   Economics defines these as **land, labour and capital**. Land includes mineral wealth (and also covers the sea!); labour includes all relevant skills and input; and capital consists of accrued wealth available for investment. Only the combination of these, by the *entrepreneur*, can give *productivity*.

Fair Trading Act 1973   Established the **Office of Fair Trading** and the **Monopolies and Mergers Commission**, with the overall responsibilities of seeing that *monopolists* do not abuse their position of strength in the market. The exemption given to the bus and coach industry was removed by the Transport Act 1985.

Financial Year   Company accounts must be made up to a 12 month period, which may end at any convenient date. The government's financial year ends on 31 March, but for many transport firms with a marked seasonal peak, it is convenient to end the financial year in the autumn.

Fixed cost   sometimes called indirect costs. Those costs that do not vary according to the level of output, in the short term. The standard example in a railway would be 'track terminals and signalling'.

Forked tariff (tarification fourchette)   A system to be found in some continental countries, where an attempt is made to impose price control of road goods transport by setting minimum and maximum rates. It proves difficult to enforce.

Fringe benefits   Rewards over and above the payment of salaries or wages that enable a company to remain competitive in the labour market. Thus banks offer mortgages to employees at low rates of interest, and railways offer free or reduced rate travel (to members of staff and their families). The most controversial example is the company car whose subsidization in this way leads to serious distortions in the market. Wherever possible, fringe benefits are assessed and taxed as if they were personal income.

Generated traffic   Traffic arising where *effective demand* is stimulated by lower prices and/or increases in the quality of service. Railway companies in the 1930s seem to have ignored it when assessing schemes for electrification, but experience suggests that much of the traffic generated by post-war investment arose from new rolling stock and/or the introduction of regular headway services rather than from electrification (the 'sparks effect') itself. Problems arise when local authorities subsidize pensioners etc in identifying the value to the operator(s) of the additional traffic thus generated.

Generic need   A marketing term defining the overall satisfactions available from a range of *substitutes*. Thus road, rail, air and sea (ferry) services each offer a partial satisfaction of the *effective demand* that arises from the generic need to travel.

Goodwill   The payment made when acquiring a 'going concern', which represents the expected *economic rent*. It is usually computed as a specific number of past years' profit. It may also be seen as a payment for the potential *economies of scope* expected to follow from the merger.

Gross National Product (GNP)   A summation of the total net output of the nation's productive economic activity. Very hard to calculate, it has been called 'Gross Naive Proximation'.

Historic costs   The costs that were incurred when a past investment was made. *Depreciation* seeks to ensure that assets thus obtained can be replaced in due course out of income, but problems arise when *current costs* are substantially greater, either through *inflation* or because of technological change that has made it impossible for a like-for-like replacement to be made.

Holding company   A company that controls one or more subsidiaries through outright ownership of their *equity capital* or by ownership of a majority of the *ordinary shares* in each one. There are a number of examples in shipping and road transport, and they are subject to the provisions of the *Fair Trading Act*. Holding companies such as Firstgroup, Go Ahead, National Express and Stagecoach will have interests in more than one mode of transport, and in a number of countries.

Horizontal integration   A consequence of a merger designed to achieve *economies of scale* or of *scope*.

Imperfect competition   See *perfect competition*.

Income elasticity of demand   *Elasticity* that varies according to the consumer's income – eg demand for public transport tends to become more elastic as people's income rises and they can afford to run a car. (Note – it is not necessary to become very wealthy for this to come into effect.) See Appendix 1.

Indivisibilities   Costs that cannot readily be *allocated*, because the use of the investment concerned is shared among a number of users. Thus the costs of building a multi-carriageway road are greater than those of building a single carriageway, but there is no way in which the additional costs can be apportioned among the users.

Inflation   Although debate continues as to its cause, it is simply defined as a process of steadily rising prices that leads to a reduction in the purchasing power of a given amount of money. It adds a further complication to the assessment of *investment*, and when it reaches the rate known as hyper-inflation it makes rational decision making virtually impossible.

Integration See *horizontal* and *vertical* integration; also *co ordination.* To integrate transport services under the ownership and/or control of a single authority is unlikely to produce benefits by way of *economies of scale,* and any advantages from *economies of scope* are likely to benefit only the operator – being in any case a one-off and fleeting advantage. It is difficult to see how the consumer stands to gain.

Interest A measure of the rate of return on capital invested, normally in the acquisition of assets (eg ships, vehicles or aircraft). It is thus a way of measuring the earnings of the firm's assets, which should be at least as much as their value could obtain were they to be sold off, and the proceeds invested at the current bank rate. It is the *net* rate of return, after deducting appropriate costs. Roughly speaking, earnings above bank rate count as *economic rent,* and any shortfall from bank rank that is allowed to continue is a measure of 'non-monetary satisfactions', or of a hope that earnings will increase in the future.

Inventory costs These are the expenses involved in holding 'an inventory of stocks'. They are intended to be minimised by *JIT,* but it has always been wise practice to keep them as low as possible, since they do not represent any immediate *cash flow.* But to cut certain stocks too much can cause 'down-time', when vehicles are not available for traffic, so to some extent inventory costs represent a form of insurance. Freight transport's customers will pay a premium where their own inventory costs are high (eg diamond merchants), which accounts for the prices chargeable for air freight. As well as the value of stocks held (which is an *opportunity cost)* there are the expenses involved in providing, insuring and maintaining buildings, and in employing staff.

Investment The expenditure of money to acquire an asset, such as a vehicle, or to improve an existing one, such as electrifying a railway. Since its success or failure turns upon the *cash flow* it is expected to generate in the unknown future, the art of forecasting demand and operating cost is central to prudent decision making. The concept of *discount* is used to narrow as far as possible the element of guessing that ultimately applies to all investment decisions. See Figure 1.1.

JIT (Just In Time) A technique for ensuring that all requirements for the productive process are delivered at (or just before) the moment when they are needed, thereby (in theory) reducing *inventory costs* to an absolute minimum. Commonly used (and misused) in manufacturing, its application to transport arises from the logistics of providing services for the movement of freight or passengers.

Joint costs   These arise where it is in the nature of the productive process that two (or more) goods or services are produced from the same *factor* input. The standard example is meat and wool from sheep-raising, but the best transport example is the relationship between the outward and return journey. This gives rise to the 'back-load' problem, when the carrier is tempted to offer a price below the going rate because the vehicle has otherwise to return empty.

Labour costs and expenses   Labour costs consist of wages and salaries; labour expenses is a term sometimes used to indicate the additional items that arise from the employment of staff, such as the administration of PAYE and NIC deductions, any further insurance requirements, etc. Items such as company cars, free or privilege travel etc should appear as fringe benefits, which are in effect additional wage costs, being taxable. Canteen facilities and the provision of sports grounds etc appear as central overheads (but Luncheon Vouchers are a fringe benefit).

Labour-intensive   A term used to describe a firm or industry in which the *factor* input of labour is disproportionately greater than that of capital (or land). Transport tends to be labour-intensive, but to a degree that varies considerably between modes.

Labour turnover   The number of people leaving a firm's employment, and being replaced, over a given period, normally 12 months,
expressed as a percentage of the total number employed. A high
labour turnover is a serious disadvantage for a firm in a service
industry like transport.

Liquid assets   Cash and bank deposits, and any asset that can be
quickly transformed into cash.

Liquidation   The process of turning all the firm's assets into cash,
as part of *winding-up*.

Liquidity ratio   The ratio of *liquid assets* to the current liabilities
of a business. A crude indicator of its solvency.

Load factor   A measure of the proportion of output actually sold.
(Seat/miles or capacity/tonne/miles measure output; passenger/
miles or loaded/tonne/miles measure sales.) A load factor for a
firm, service or journey would be expressed as:

$$\frac{passenger/miles}{seat\ miles} \times 100$$

Location theory   A body of theory on the boundary of economics
and geography that attempts to explain and thus to predict the location of firms, transport costs being one of the variables considered.

Logistics   The processes involved in controlling the manufacture
of goods and/or services. It will include supply chain management,
physical distribution management, and the positioning and movement of assets. While it requires effective provision of transport, it
is also the process of control necessary for the provision of the
transport service.

Long-run marginal cost   The additional cost of a marginal unit
of demand when there is no immediate limit to the capacity of
output because of a high level of *sunk cost*. It is considered desirable
as a basis for pricing in the case of roads, bridges etc, but would

lead to rapid insolvency if used to price the movement function. And as Keynes remarked, 'in the long run, we are all dead'.

Marginal cost   See *Long-run* and *Short-run* marginal cost.

Marginal cost pricing   A policy that sets prices equal to *marginal costs* (insofar as these can be effectively known). It has been recommended as being appropriate for nationalized industries, where *short-run costs* would be the basis of pricing, on the grounds that the practice would maximize economic welfare. It is however difficult to reconcile such a policy with the requirement of satisfying a *test rate of return*. See *Long-run marginal cost* for pricing of investment with high levels of *sunk cost*.

Market pricing   A policy that sets prices so as to achieve the highest level of net *cash flow* that the market will permit without driving away custom that makes a contribution (see *contributory revenue*). The 'floor' price is such that, for a given quantum of output, revenue covers *avoidable cost*, while the 'ceiling' is set by the prices of competitors. (Hence 'charging what the traffic will bear' was discouraged when railways had a substantial element of *monopoly*.) 'At the end of the day', average revenue must still exceed *average costs*.

Money   Anything that will be accepted as a means of discharging a debt. In primitive economies, what passes for money will have intrinsic value (cattle, cigarettes, gold etc), but in advanced economies money is effectively a claim on some acceptable authority – coins and notes on the government, cheques, credit cards etc on banks or other sources of credit (including, in the case of 'store cards', the creditor!). The three standard functions of money are: (1) a medium of exchange; (2) a unit of account; (3) a store of value. It will be seen that these are interlocked, and that they function less and less well as *inflation* erodes them.

Monopoly   A state of affairs in which there is a single producer (or, within limits, a single seller) of a product for which there is no acceptable *substitute*. Thus the railways have never had a monopoly of the market for the movement of goods or passengers, although for a century or so they were in a dominant position. If only one bus company were permitted to operate in a city it still would not have a monopoly because of the alternative of other modes, including walking. Monopolists were thought to pursue maximization of *profit* until recent work has suggested that the objective of firms in a monopoly situation may be *satisficing*.

Monopoly profit   An example of *economic rent* arising from the ability of a firm in a monopoly situation to extract higher prices than would be possible were the market to be acting as a constraint. In certain types of *cross-subsidy* a firm will have to extract monopoly profit (if it can) from one part of its business in order to balance an outright loss elsewhere. This is generally regarded as undesirable.

Monopsony   A state of affairs in which there is a single buyer of a given product or service, who can then use this power, within limits, to set prices and conditions (the limit being the point at which sellers decide to withhold their offer, and move to a different market). At one time the nationalized airlines had a substantial element of monopsony in the employment of qualified cockpit staff.

Natural monopoly   In a situation where *economies of scale* are such that a single firm can produce at lower *average cost* than a number of firms could, there will be a tendency for firms to combine until there is a single monopolist. In the early 20th century this was seen to apply to the telephone service, and later on, with the growth of distribution grids, to gas and electricity. It was also probably true of railways up to the establishment of commercial motor transport. Government response has been to encourage single ownership, at first in public hands, but more recently in private hands, with a 'watchdog', or regulator. But it is clear that technology can undermine a natural monopoly, as it has in telecommunications, thus requiring government, in the teeth of opposition from *vested interest*, to dismantle the monopolistic structure of the industry concerned.

Net present value (NPV)   As an alternative to *discounted cash flow* (*DCF*), the value of all predicted future costs and benefits is discounted to provide a 'realistic' figure in terms of *current cost*. If the result is greater than the investment required it may be considered worthwhile.

Network subsidy The practice in which a local authority enters into an agreement with a transport operator to make up any short-fall of revenue arising from the provision of a defined network of services. It differs from *deficit financing* in being agreed in advance. It was introduced as an alternative to *cross-subsidy*, but has the disadvantage of weakening the operator's incentive to maximize efficiency.

Obsolescence Consumer demand is highly subjective, and when innovation produces an acceptable *substitute* an established product or service may become 'out of date', as for example happened when the ballpoint pen reduced the demand for pen nibs virtually to nothing. The development of reliable motor buses for urban tran-sport in the late 1920s made tramcars with a further 20 years of mechanical usefulness obsolete, partly because the tramcars had been 'built to last', and so had become visually out of date in passengers' eyes as well.

Oligopoly A state of affairs in which a small number of firms dominate supply (as came about after 1945 in the UK motor car industry). Unlike in monopoly, where there is reasonable certainty about the way the monopolist will behave (profit-maximizing or *satisficing*), firms in an oligopoly situation, who continue to com-pete, may do so by way of price, product differentiation, or promo-tion. A frequent outcome however is the development of a *cartel*.

Opportunity cost One of the most important concepts in econ-omics, this turns upon the statement that a benefit forgone is a loss. The opportunity cost of a garage is the difference between its value to the firm in its present use and the price that it would fetch on the market (providing that is the greater), combined with the cost of buying alternative accommodation (providing it is cheaper). A railway might calculate the opportunity costs of its city-centre carriage sidings by assessing their site value, and deducting the cost of buying and developing a 'green field' site, including the extra *positioning mileage*. If the result is positive, an opportunity cost exists that could be escaped. Many transport investments, such as railway tunnels, have no alternative use and therefore involve no opportunity cost.

Ordinary shares   See *equity capital*.

Pareto optimum   See *economic efficiency*.

Passenger service obligation (PSO)   Before 1974 British Rail was paid a subvention in respect of shortfall of revenue against the cost of providing services that the Board wished to withdraw. Under the Railways Act of that year, which brought UK practice in line with that of the *EC*, this was replaced with a contract to provide a defined set of operations (sometimes called the 'social railway'), in return for an agreed annual sum. The system may be likened to *network subsidy*.

Payback period   The period over which it is forecast that cumulative net revenue will amount to a sum equal to that originally invested. A very crude measure, it does not allow for an element of *profit*, nor for the effects of *inflation* or *discount*. For all but small and short-run projects it is better to use *net present value* or *discounted cash flow* for the evaluation of a proposed investment.

Perceived costs   The cost of any purchase as perceived by the customer is highly subjective. In the case of transport costs this is complicated by the weakness of the price mechanism in many inputs (see *road-use pricing*). But whereas it is hard to underestimate the price paid for a bus or train journey, all evidence, as well as personal experience, shows that motorists consistently underestimate the cost of a car journey. It has not been uncommon for manufacturers to underestimate their transport costs, especially in the case of own-account operation.

Perfect competition   A notional situation in which certain highly artificial circumstances are supposed to hold good: large numbers of sellers and buyers, complete freedom of entry to and exit from the market, a homogeneous product as perceived by the consumer, the absence of economies of scale, and perfect knowledge of current prices among all parties. Markets may approach perfection (tramp shipping and an unregulated taxi market are possible examples). It is assumed that in circumstances of perfect competition, price = *short-run marginal cost*.

Positioning mileage   Journeys necessitated to get a vehicle into position to commence a remunerative trip incur zero *avoidable cost*, and any traffic they may be able to attract will provide valuable *contributory revenue*.

Preference shares   Shares requiring payment of interest as priority over *ordinary shares*, which will not normally carry voting rights. See *equity capital*.

Price discrimination   An example of *market pricing*, in which the level of charge is not directly related to costs. A standard example is the tariff for electricity for night storage heaters, where the producer cuts the price because night-time demand does not take up all the capacity that is inescapably available. It is common among passenger transport operators in times of low (off-peak) demand, when extra traffic that helps to maximize *cash flow* is welcome, provided it exceeds *avoidable cost* – note that, within a guaranteed day, wages are not avoidable. But it is also possible to base prices on the off-peak, and discriminate against peak demand. Railway fares (in almost every country in the world) discriminate between first and standard class passengers, which is an example of segmenting the market and discriminating by segment. (Few railways have found it worth segmenting supply beyond two classes; there are extra costs involved.) Discrimination by segment is related to varying *elasticities of demand*, and while it is almost unknown in bus transport it is undoubtedly practised in coach hire and in road freight transport and distribution. It is the basis of airline charging, and is an ancient practice in shipping.

Price elasticity of demand   A measure of customers' response to changes in price, expressed as:

$$\frac{\%\ \text{change in demand}}{\%\ \text{change in price}}$$

If demand is **elastic** the figure will be greater than 1, in which case a price rise will drive traffic away more quickly than it would if the figure is less than 1, when demand is said to be **inelastic**. (Elasticity of demand for bus passengers is said to be around +3, but this is a national figure, and there are certainly local and/or regional variants.) Elasticity is one of the most important concepts in economics, but it is not easily estimated until after the event (by when it may be too late!).

Private costs   Costs actually and necessarily incurred, excluding *externalities.*

Product differentiation   Firms in competition may try to emphasize the special qualities of their service, rather than compete entirely on price. The difference may be more apparent than real. There is also evidence from confectionery and household detergents that a firm can maximize net cash flow by differentiating its own product, even though the difference between two chocolate bars can be small. Some bus companies find that it pays to keep subsidiaries trading alongside the parent firm, in a different livery.

Production   Transport, like all industries, is in the business of combining the *factors of production* to offer a consumable product, which in its simplest form is defined as 'safe arrival' or 'safe delivery'. Output is measured in seat/miles or capacity tonne/miles (see *load factor).* But, as is the case in most service industries, output cannot be stored, perishing in the moment of production. If for no other reason, this is why pricing is all-important.

Productivity The output of the firm measured against a given input of one of the *factors of production* (the others being held constant). Most often discussed in terms of **productivity of labour**, which will increase if output rises with or without a reduction in staff.

Profit   In very simple terms, net revenue after deducting all costs incurred, including *depreciation*. Accountants distinguish **gross profit** (in effect, the *money* left after making all payments necessary for the firm to continue to trade), and **net profit** (being gross profit less interest on loans and depreciation). Net profit is sometimes called 'profit before tax'. In economics we distinguish between **normal profit**, which is what is left after meeting the *opportunity costs of all factor inputs*, and which is just sufficient to keep the firm trading in the market it is in, when greater returns may be available elsewhere; and supernormal profit, which is any return greater than that. (The concept of super-normal profit is close to that of *economic rent*.) See also *monopoly profit*.

Public choice theory   The analysis of administrative behaviour in terms of individual expectations. Thus elected or appointed individuals or committees will be tempted to choose public goods or forms of regulation in accordance with their own preferences, rather than the supposed objective of 'the public good' (however impossible it may be to define that outcome). In addition, they will tend to promote their own agenda, in a form of satisficing, at the expense of optimal public expenditure.

Public goods   *See collective goods.*

Real terms   A series of figures that have been adjusted to allow for *inflation* form a better means of judging their significance than the actual figures would. It is usual to take a specific year as the base, which may be the current year ('in 2002 terms') or a convenient year in the past ('expressed in 1998 prices').

Regulation   Because transport is a 'fail-dangerous' activity, and an industry whose product cannot be assessed in advance by a prospective purchaser, it is necessary for the state to regulate its **quality**. Such regulation, while it imposes a cost on all firms, and may discourage innovation, does not discriminate between different operators (note the use of the word 'discriminate' here in a different context from that of pricing). When however regulation extends to imposing barriers to entry (see *contestability*) it confers privileges on those who are 'inside', and is thus markedly discriminatory; this is called **quantity regulation**. Where there is an element of *monopoly*, which may follow from the imposition of quantity regulation, it is often thought necessary to prevent firms from abusing their monopoly power, in which case there will be a system of **regulation of prices**. (The three terms are often spoken of as *quality control, quantity control* and *price control*.) Note that 'deregulation' invariably means the removal of quantity and price control only.

Road pricing Because of the way roads are paid for, out of the total government funds available, there is no payment to be made at the point of use. Thus we say that the use of the road incurs zero marginal cost to the user. In this situation there is no incentive to 'economize' in their use, as we do when we are subject to a 'unit price', as in the case of our consumption of gas and electricity (nonmetered water is also an example of zero marginal cost to the consumer). It was proposed by the Smeed Report in 1964 that road use should be priced by way of an electronic meter in the vehicle, thereby bringing home to the user the costs that arise from congestion, and encouraging the more economical use of scarce road space.

Satisficing In simple terms we would expect a businessperson to seek maximum profit, but it has been observed that the divorce of ownership and control that is characteristic of the large businesses that have grown up since the 1920s can mean that the managers have a different objective, whatever the shareholders may want. (This difference appeared quite early in the history of railways.) If then the strategic objectives of managers are different from those of the multitude of shareholders, who individually have little power, the managers are said to be satisficing. Thus they may put growth above maximum profit, if it increases their status and power, or they may be ready to negotiate for the creation of a *cartel*. Since *economic efficiency* may be said to depend upon the profit motive, it is a concern in developed economies that growth may impede prosperity. But no one knows quite what to do about it.

Scarcity   Economics is not concerned with 'free goods', such as air under normal circumstances (compressed air is another matter). One definition of economics relates to its concern with the efficient allocation of scarce resources (see *economic efficiency*). It is central to its study to note that prices are related to relative scarcity at least as much as they are to costs of production. Thus transport has become steadily cheaper (in *real terms*) as it has become more readily available.

Service industries   All industries have a product. In manufacturing it is said to be 'durable'. A service, whether it is catering, legal advice, or hairdressing, is a perishable product, that cannot be stored. One consequence of this is the special importance of the staff – a factory can stock up and survive a strike, but a railway cannot.

Short-run marginal cost   The additional cost of a marginal unit of demand when capacity is relatively inflexible, all other things being equal. It is stated to be the price that rules in circumstances of *perfect competition*. See *marginal cost pricing*. While it is useful to know the short-run marginal cost of output, for many pricing decisions, it is of no use in reaching decisions on *investment*.

Social costs   The total cost to the community of any economic activity include both *private costs* and *externalities*. In the absence of some form of *road pricing* the *social costs* of private motoring substantially exceed the *private costs*. The same can be said of many transport investments – see *social cost/benefit analysis*.

Social cost/benefit analysis   A technique which attempts to measure the total costs and benefits of an investment (or disinvestment), allowing for *discount*. There have been a number of controversial examples over the past 50 years, including the M1 Motorway, the Victoria Line, the Cambrian Coast Line (an example of disinvestment), the Roskill Commission on the site for a third London Airport, and the Cooper Report on the Channel Tunnel. Many economists are highly suspicious of the technique, since (1) it is extremely sophisticated, yet the data it uses must be hypothetical; (2) because of its sophistication it is open to manipulation and can

224 | Appendix 2

produce results in line with the conclusion that clients, usually politicians, might prefer; (3) it makes no allowance for the distribution effects – ie, the relative advantage of winners and losers. The Roskill Report is also famous for its choice of site being totally rejected, in favour of Stansted, which had been the site preferred by civil servants ever since 1945.

Standard charging   A policy that sets prices to the customer at a standard rate, irrespective of either *marginal costs* or *demand elasticities*. One example is sometimes called 'postalization', when the price is the same for all consignments, as with the letter post; another example of this is a 'flat fare' for all journeys within a specified area. Alternatively it is a price based solely on mileage with or without a 'taper' over longer distances that may roughly reflect falling marginal costs. It necessarily implies *cross-subsidization*, since it ignores the subjectivity of demand, whereby a given trip or consignment may be valued more by one customer than another (in which case one may be charged 'too much' and another 'too little'; in the latter case *consumer surplus* will be present). See also *market pricing* and *price discrimination*.

Substitutes   Some goods are perceived as filling much the same need, the standard example being (for most though not all consumers) butter and margarine, which would be called 'close substitutes'. Railway managers for too long thought they had a monopoly, ignoring the growth of commercial motor transport as a substitute; bus managers similarly failed to recognize the private car as a substitute for their services. Substitutability is a highly subjective matter, and in transport it is important to remember that, in the longer run, anything may be a substitute for anything else. Someone may decide to watch TV instead of going to the pictures – that is a close substitute. Or the person may decide to watch TV instead of going to the pub – that may not seem so close, but it has the same effect on demand for bus services. A change in the price of one substitute will affect demand for the other – see Appendix 1, *cross-elasticity*.

Sunk costs   The costs of *investment* where (1) there is little *opportunity cost* (eg a tube railway tunnel) and/or (2) the *payback period* is so long that *long-run marginal costs* are low (as with a tanker) or even negligible (eg a new bridge). Failure to earn *interest* on investments of this kind may not mean closure or insolvency – a tube railway may continue to produce a net positive *cash flow*, even if it is insufficient to service its *capital*; a tanker may be subject to 'slow steaming' or may be laid up, in the hope of better freights in due course, rather than being scrapped because its earnings fail to cover part or all of the return expected when it was decided to invest.

Super-normal profit   See *profit*.

Supply-side subsidy   Subsidy paid to a producer of transport, generally by way of *deficit financing, network subsidy* or in response to *tendering*. Its effect is to substitute the subsidizing authority for the individual as the firm's customer. It is often criticized for weakening the incentive of management to seek out and satisfy demand in the market. *Public choice theory* indicates certain weaknesses inherent in this policy.

Tendering   A process whereby public authorities seek to obtain the best bargain they can for the provision of a service considered to be socially or politically justified, that has not been provided in the market. It is a form of providing for *supply-side subsidy*, but because it is usually on a small scale it is considered to distort the market less than *deficit financing* or *network subsidy*. Note that network subsidy may be arranged through a process of tendering.

Test rate of discount   *Capital* invested by government and nationalized industries has an *opportunity cost* like any other, and in the 1960s the Treasury became concerned about misallocation arising from investment in assets that might not yield a satisfactory rate of return. (They had before them the wastefulness of much investment in British Railways under the Modernisation Plan in the 1950s.) All such investment has to satisfy a discounted rate of return, using a figure provided from time to time by the Treasury, expressed in *real terms* – eg, a test rate of 8% would appear as 13%

if inflation was expected to amount to 5%. At best, a rather crude measure of opportunity cost (as to which the going rate in the private sector would be the criterion), it has tended to be manipulated for political ends, in the light of contemporary monetary policy.

Total costs   Often taken to be the costs incurred by the firm which, having been set against revenue, leave a margin of *profit*. In this sense they must include a satisfactory return on *capital*, and, in the case of a sole trader, an item representing the proprietor's input as manager. See *average costs*.

Transfer payments   Where money is taken from one person or class of persons and used to benefit another, it is a transfer. Income tax combined with the provision of *public goods* tends to transfer from the rich to the poor; a poll tax tends to do the opposite. 'Vicious' *cross-subsidy* is a form of transfer payment.

Transparent subsidy   Subsidy is said to be transparent when it is possible to calculate some form of specific benefit by way of return. *Tendering* is a way of maximizing transparency, which is difficult to achieve in the case of *network subsidy* and is totally absent from *deficit financing*.

User subsidy   Subsidy paid to individual users of a service who are considered worthy of merit, examples being 'senior citizens' and those with special needs. It is considered preferable to *supply-side subsidy* because by boosting the user's purchasing power it does not weaken the incentive of managers to seek out and satisfy demand in the market. It creates problems, by (1) imposing costs in order to identify the indebtedness of the subsidizing authority, and (2) requiring an estimate to be made of the quantity of *generated traffic*. Opinions differ as to the optimum technique for providing the subsidy, some advocating identity cards, others 'smart cards', and yet others the use of tokens. It has been shown that user subsidy is effective in preventing special groups from effectively diverting supply-side subsidy to their own interests.

Utility A very important economic concept, denoting the desirability of a particular satisfaction as subjectively determined by the consumer (at a given level of price and quality). The marginal utility of two potential purchases will decide which of them attracts our next expenditure. Marginal utility has the great significance of recognizing that 'value' is subjectively determined, and is not inherent in the commodity. It put an end to the use of the 'labour theory of value', and finally undermined mercantilism.

Value judgement A preconceived idea that should not be allowed to override objective decision making, though it can have a place after the true costs of decision have been calculated. Thus a deliberate policy that favoured rural transport at the expense of urban would derive from a value judgement, that rural life is in some way 'better' than urban. A *transfer payment* that favours the poor at the expense of the rich may not be entirely a value judgement, since over-wide differences in wealth may prevent the market from securing *economic efficiency*.

Variable costs Sometimes called 'direct costs'. Those that vary with the level of output. In transport the cost of fuel is a clear example. *Labour,* on the other hand, must be judged according to circumstances: wages may be a *fixed cost* within a guaranteed day or other period, but will be variable in the longer run (see *avoidable costs).* Salaries are generally regarded as part of the fixed central costs of the firm, but will be variable in the still longer run. Costing thus requires careful thought so as to identify the reasons why we need to know our costs, and the length of time with which we are concerned.

Vertical integration A consequence of a merger usually intended to improve managerial control of costs and/or sales, eg an airline buying control of a chain of travel agencies. The separation of Railtrack from the Train Operating Companies broke the traditional vertical integration of the railways in Great Britain.

Vested interest Management may have a vested interest in the growth of the firm, even if one consequence is lower *profits* for the shareholders. Road staff may have a vested interest in restrictive practices, even if they work to the disadvantage of customers. Civil servants may have a vested interest in *regulation,* if its removal threatens their employment. There is perhaps no greater barrier to progress and *economic efficiency.* (Clearly everyone concerned has a vested interest in the success of the firm, but the term is rarely used in that sense.)

Winding up   The process by which a firm's life is brought to an end, either because the *equity* shareholders wish it to cease trading or on account of its insolvency. In the latter case it may still be voluntary, or it may be the result of a court order. In all cases it is preceded by *liquidation.*

Working capital   Defined as net current assets minus current liabilities (debts, taxes etc outstanding, wages and salaries due, debentures, issued shares, etc). In setting up a business it is the amount of money needed to be invested over and above that required for the purchase of its fixed assets (property, vehicles etc). This is required in order to cover liabilities incurred, such as purchases of fuel, in respect of which the revenue will arise later. It may thus include credit (see *money*).

X-efficiency   The efficiency with which a firm combines *factor* inputs to attain its own objectives. Only if these are profit-maximizing can it be assumed that the outcome of its production process will ensure *economic efficiency.*

Zero marginal cost   A state of affairs in which consumers' costs are either met by payment in advance (as with a travel card), or through taxation (as with the provision of roads). In such cases no price is payable at the moment of consumption or purchase of the services or goods concerned, and the consumer therefore has no incentive to economize in the use of the *factor* inputs required for their production; factor allocation, and thus *economic efficiency,* are thus likely to be distorted. See *road pricing.*

Appendix 3

Sources of further information

BOOKS

Banister, D and Button, K (eds) (1991) *Transport in a Free Market Economy*, Macmillan, Basingstoke

Beesley, ME (ed) (1997) *Privatization, Regulation and Deregulation*, 2nd edn, Routledge, London

Beesley, ME (ed) (1998) *Regulating Utilities: Understanding the issues*, Institute of Economic Affairs in association with London Business School

Beesley, ME (ed) (1999) *Regulating Utilities: A new era?* Institute of Economic Affairs in association with London Business School

Button, K (1993) *Transport, the Environment and Economic Policy*, Edward Elgar, Cheltenham

Button, K (1993) *Transport Economics*, 2nd edn, Edward Elgar, Cheltenham

Cole, S (1998) *Applied Transport Economics: Policy, management and decision making*, 2nd edn, Kogan Page, London

Glaister, S, Burnham, J, Stevens, H and Travers, A (1998) *Transport Policy in Britain*, Macmillan, Basingstoke

Gubbins, E J (1996) *Managing Transport Operations*, 2nd edn, Kogan Page, London

Hensher, DA and Brewer, AM (2001) *Transport: An economics and management perspective*, Oxford University Press, Oxford

Hibbs, J (1989) *Marketing Management in the Bus and Coach Industry*, Croner, Kingston upon Thames

Hibbs, J (2000) *An Introduction to Transport Studies*, 3rd edn, Kogan Page, London

Middleton, VTC (1988) *Marketing in Travel and Tourism*, Heinemann, London

Nash, C A (1982) *Economics of Public Transport*, Longman, London

Page, SJ (1999) *Transport and Tourism*, Longman, London

Parker, D and Stacey, R (1994) *Chaos, Management and Economics*, Institute of Economic Affairs, London

Riley, D (2001) *Taken for a Ride: Trains, taxpayers and the Treasury*, Centre for Land Policy Studies, London

Roth, G (1998) *Roads in a Market Economy*, 2nd edn, Avebury Technical, Aldershot

Self, P (1993) *Government by the Market? The politics of public choice*, Macmillan, Basingstoke

Shaw, SJ (1993) *Transport Strategy and Policy*, Blackwell, Oxford

Tolley, R and Turton, B (? date) *Transport Systems, Policy and Planning: A geographical approach*, Longmans, London

Truelove, P (1992) *Decision Making in Transport Planning*, Longman, London

Tullock, G, Seldon, A and Brady, GL (2000) *Government: Whose obedient servant?* Institute of Economic Affairs, London

White, P (2002) *Public Transport: Its planning, management and operation*, 4th edn, Spon Press, London

Note: Reference to the term catallactics will be found on page 338 of Roll, A (1973) *A History of Economic Thought*, Faber & Faber, London

WEB SITES

Note: The Web sites of single-issue non-government organizations should be treated with reserve, since the material they present may not be entirely disinterested. The following sites are recommended:

Adam Smith Institute: www.adamsmith.org
    The Adam Smith Institute is one of Britain's leading innovators of market economic policies. It has been part of a worldwide movement toward free markets and free trade. The Institute's main focus has been to introduce choice and competition, extending the influence of free markets in giving ordinary people the chance to help frame their future by their choices, and redesigning public services in ways that inject innovation and customer responsiveness into their delivery.
Automobile Association: www.theaa.com
Centre for European Policy Studies: www.ceps.be
    CEPS is an independent research group with staff from 15 countries, aiming to produce sound policy research leading to constructive solutions to the challenges facing Europe.
Commission for Integrated Transport: www.cfit.gov.uk
Confederation of Passenger Transport UK: www.cpt-uk.org/cpt
Demos: www.demos.co.uk
    Demos is an independent think-tank and research institute. Its role is to help reinvigorate public policy and political thinking, and to develop radical solutions to long-term problems.
Department for Transport: www.dft.gov.uk
European Commission Representation in the United Kingdom: www.cec.org.uk
European Union: www.europa.eu.int
Freight Transport Association: www.fta.co.uk
Her Majesty's Treasury: www.hm-treasury.gov.uk
Institute of Economic Affairs (IEA): www.iea.org.uk
    The IEA was established in 1955 and its mission is to improve understanding of the fundamental institutions of a free society with particular reference to the role of markets in solving economic and social problems.

Road Haulage Association: www.rha.net
Society of Motor Manufacturers and Traders: www.smmt.co.uk
Town and Country Planning Association: www.tcpa.org.uk

JOURNALS AND PERIODICALS

Transport journals

Distribution Business (UK Transport Press) 10 issues yearly
H&T (Institution of Highways and Transportation) 10 issues yearly
International Journal of Transport Management (Pergamon/Institute
   of Logistics and Transport) Twice yearly
Jane's Urban Transport Systems (Jane's Information Group) Annual
Jane's World Railways (Jane's Information Group) Annual
Journal of Transport Economics and Policy (University of Bath) Three
   issues yearly
Logistics & Transport Focus (Institute of Logistics and Transport) 11
   issues yearly
Transport Law and Policy Journal (Waterfront Group) Monthly
Transport Reviews (Taylor & Francis) Quarterly

Magazines and newspapers

Bus and Coach Professional (Partnership Publishing) Monthly
Cargo Systems (Informa Business Publishing) Monthly
Cargo Tomorrow (ICHCA) Six issues yearly
CBW Coach and Bus Week (EMAP Automotive) Weekly
Community Transport (Community Transport Association) Six issues
   yearly
Containerisation International (Informa UK) Monthly
Freight (Freight Transport Association) Monthly
Freight Industry Times (McMillan Scott) Quarterly
Going Green (Environmental Transport Association) Quarterly
International Freighting Weekly (Informa UK) Weekly
Local Transport Today (Landor Publishing) 26 issues yearly
Modern Railways (Ian Allan Publishing) Monthly
Motor Industry Management (Institute of the Motor Industry) 10
   issues yearly

Motor Transport (Reed Business Information) Weekly

Planning (Haymarket Business Publications/Royal Town Planning Institute) Weekly

Rail (EMAP Active Outdoor) 26 issues yearly

Rail Express (Foursight Publications) Monthly

Railnews (Railnews) Monthly

Rail Professional (Institution of Railway Operators) Monthly

Railwatch (Railway Development Society) Quarterly

The Railway (IPC Country and Leisure Media) Monthly

Railway Gazette International (Reed Business Information) Monthly

Railway Strategies (Hartford Publications) Quarterly

Roadway (Road Haulage Association) Monthly

TEC Traffic Engineering & Control (Hemming Group) 11 issues yearly

Traffic World (Journal of Commerce) Weekly

Tramways & Urban Transit (Ian Allan Publishing/Light Rail Transit Association) Monthly

Transit (Landor Publishing) 26 issues yearly

Transport News (KAV Publicity) Monthly

Transport News Digest (Transport Press Services) Monthly

Transport Report (Transport 2000) Quarterly

Travel & Tourism Analyst (Mintel International Group) Six issues yearly

TRANSPORT POLICY SOURCES

National voluntary organizations

National Federation of Bus Users, PO Box 320, Portsmouth PO5 3SD

Railway Development Society, Roman House, 9–10 College Terrace, London E3 5AN

Transport 2000, Walkden House, 10 Melton Street, London NW1 3EJ

Trade associations

Association of Train Operating Companies (ATOC), 40 Bernard
Street, London WC1N 1BY

Confederation of Passenger Transport UK (CPT), Imperial House,
15–19 Kingsway, London WC2B 6UN

Freight Transport Association (FTA), Hermes House, St John's
Road, Tunbridge Wells, Kent TN4 9UZ

Society of Motor Manufacturers and Traders (SMMT), Forbes
House, Halkin Street, London WC2H 7BN

Professional bodies

Institute of Highways and Transportation, 3 Lygon Place, Ebury
Street, London SW1W 0JS

Institute of Logistics and Transport, 11/12 Buckingham Gate,
London SW1E 6LB

Institute of the Motor Industry, Fanshaws, Brickendon, Hertford
SG13 8PQ

Institute of Railway Studies, National Railway Museum, Leeman
Road, York Y26 4XJ

Institute of Transport Administration, Mill House, 11 Nightingale
Road, Horsham, Sussex RH12 2NW

Road Haulage Association (RHA), Roadway House, 35 Monument
Hill, Weybridge, Surrey KT33 8RN

Index